THE DAILY *Burn*

A Daily Guitar Practice Program for the Development of Accuracy, Dexterity, Strength, and Speed

CHRIS COTTER

ISBN: 978-0-6922804-2-3

www.jamestownguitars.com

This book is dedicated to my first guitar instructor Robert L. Jones, for opening the door to what would become my life's work.

And to Shane Hawkins, for believing in and blessing me with the opportunity to make it a reality.

About the Author

Chris Cotter is a guitar and ensemble instructor at Infinity Visual and Performing Arts in Jamestown, NY. In 1984, he started his formal education on the guitar with his private instructor, Robert L. Jones. Over the years spent together, they developed many effective practices, including what would become the basis for this book. In addition to teaching, Chris has played in several performing and recording projects and brings 30 years of experience and expertise on the guitar to develop effective teaching, learning, and practice strategies to students of all levels. His teaching philosophy is simple: "To meet the individual where he or she is every day and act as a guide on the wonderful journey of making music on the guitar".

Acknowledgements

I would like to thank the many important people who have been instrumental in making this book a reality: Judy Cotter, for always believing. My wife Jau, who through all of the ups and downs of a musician's life, never once gave up. My son Jarren, for being the inspiration and reason for everything I do. Shane Hawkins, who put her faith in me and gave me the opportunities at Infinity. Without her support and mentorship and providing me the vehicle, the chance to do this very special and important work would never have happened. All of the instructors and staff at the Infinity Program, especially Sarah Marchitelli, Amanda Barton, T.R. McKotch, Adam Owens, Kyle Gustafson, Ken Larsen, Julie Anderson, and Jim Beal for their unending support of this idea. "The Originals" - Caelan Register, Hayley Restivo, Joshua Reuter, and Ryan Hawkins. And last, but certainly not least - Every single one of my past, current, and future students and their parents. Without you, none of this would be possible. You have all been and continue to be my greatest teachers.

Table of Contents

Introduction

Playing the guitar is a physical discipline; and like any other skill, it requires preparation and training to be done well. In this book, you will use a program that is proven to assist you in the development of proper and effective playing technique. By laying a firm foundation, with the use of a specific practice routine that you can do on a regular basis, you can be certain that you will develop the physical skills necessary to improve in every aspect of your guitar playing.

When you embark on any physical practice routine, you must first get your body into shape. Athletes spend months in the off-season getting themselves into shape, then move on to training camps where they train harder and deeper with their teams. When one joins a branch of the armed forces, he/she first goes through boot camp. Police, fire, and rescue workers must be in excellent condition. Guitar players are no exception. Many guitarists undermine their talent and never reach their true potential as players by simply neglecting the important step of getting "in shape" by developing good fundamental technique. Get the picture?

Guitar technique is one of the most widely sought after, talked about, and studied facets of guitar playing. Myriad volumes have been authored on the subject. There are countless instructional materials available to the developing guitarist. In the quest for proper guitar technique and the understanding of it, we must first develop accuracy, synchronization and strength in the hands and fingers. With this strength and accuracy comes the dexterity and speed necessary to practice, perform, and effectively bring our musical ideas to the guitar.

It is much easier to develop good technical habits at the beginning of your studies, rather than having to unlearn bad technique habits or relearn the habit of playing with good technique. Muscles develop a "memory" when they are used in repeated tasks. This is why when you learn to type on a keyboard, you first go one finger at a time. Then, as you continue to type the same words over and over, your fingers begin to "remember" where the keys are. It is the same with the guitar. Your fingers will remember how to execute something correctly and accurately with the proper practice. However, they will also remember how to do something awkwardly, sloppy, and just plain wrong.

The goal of this book is to provide you with a daily practice routine in conjunction with a practice log and progress tracking system that come together to help you to develop, improve, and maintain a firm foundation of guitar technique. This book/workbook combination is designed for guitarists of all skill levels, from the beginning student to the professional guitarist to the multi-faceted guitar instructor. This is a time-tested program that has been used by hundreds of students. Using this simple system, you will develop the "Four Pillars" of guitar technique: accuracy, dexterity, strength, and speed. You will be playing in top form, giving you the freedom to achieve your musical and guitar playing goals.

Part 1 – Getting Started

About this Book

Recommended Materials

Setting up your Workspace

Practice

About this Book

There is an old saying that "Your work is only as good as your tools." The book you are holding in your hand is a very useful tool.

The Daily Burn is not a "method book" or "learning system", but a healthy supplement for both, and is designed to be incorporated into any system of study and practice. This book is a practice routine, workbook, practice log, and progress tracking system all rolled into one complete program. It is meant to be followed in order of presentation, following all instructions. This will ensure that you achieve the most benefit from the program. Simply follow the instructions for each day, log the details of each session in the progress tracker each day as you go, and you will see great results.

The program is based entirely on practicing different combinations of synchronization exercises for the left and right hands. These are practiced in a very specific order, for a specific length of time each day, in conjunction with an intricate and very detailed speed-development plan with the use of a metronome.

For best results, you should follow the program exactly as it is written; it is designed in such a way that these combinations will work to develop the nervous system and muscular movement patterns to become more efficient and balanced. This is very important, because it is this balance that allows you to maintain your accuracy, dexterity, strength and speed at optimal levels.

The Daily Burn is exactly what it sounds like (although it doesn't really "burn"), in that it should be used daily. It is designed to be used first in your overall daily practice routine. However, there will inevitably be days when you cannot practice it. If you need to skip a day, don't worry. Just jump right in to the next day in the program and keep going. While using the program, you will see a noticeable improvement in your entire guitar practice.

By the time you complete the entire Daily Burn program, you will have refined your technique to the point of optimal accuracy, dexterity, strength, and speed. From there, all you need do is maintain it. That's it! And you will always be sure to be playing at the top of your game.

Recommended Tools and Accessories

To get the most from The Daily Burn program, you will need some accessories. These tools will help you to have effective and efficient practice sessions and to achieve the best possible results.

1. **Metronome** - A metronome is absolutely essential for this program to work. Among all of the tools that a musician can possess, the metronome is perhaps the most important. EVERY guitarist needs to own one. The entire Daily Burn program is based on practice with a metronome. It is safe to say that you cannot do this program without one. Electronic metronomes that allow you to choose the click tone, light, speed in increments of one beat, and a timer are best. There are a number of very good free apps for smartphones and computers, in addition to stand-alone, battery operated units. You don't need to spend a fortune, but get a good one. Wind-up and old-school "pendulum" type metronomes are not recommended for this program.

2. **Tuner** – You need to play in tune. An electronic tuner is the fastest way to get there. Again, you don't need to spend a lot of money here, but do get the best quality that you can afford. Because we want the Daily Burn to be a "part" of your entire practice, you will want to get in tune as quickly as possible and get to work. Save the tuning forks, pitch pipes and tuning "by ear" for later.

3. **Timer** – You will need to keep track of time, in minutes and seconds, throughout this program. Every cell phone or other hand-held device in the world has a timer. If you don't have one of these, a kitchen timer or even the clock on your wall can work. Just make sure it is accessible.

4. **Practice Chair** – This should be comfortable, adjustable for proper height, and allow you to keep good posture throughout your practice sessions. You need to be able to be relaxed and focused and you cannot do that if you are uncomfortably "hunched over" your guitar.

5. **Music Stand** – Good quality, sturdy and fully adjustable for height. You want your materials in easy view and within reach. "Conductor Style" models are best.

6. **Pencil** – So you can record your practice in the practice log and progress tracker. This is essential. You'll be doing this every day, so buy a few.

7. **A well-lit**, quiet place where you can practice undisturbed.

8. **Your guitar** – Well set up and maintained, in tune with fresh strings

9. **Guitar Picks** – These should be medium to medium-heavy gauge

10. **Amplifier** (for electric guitar players) – Play plugged in. You need to be able to hear the quality of every note you play. You cannot do this "unplugged" with an electric guitar.

11. **Guitar Stand** – You'll be putting your guitar down for frequent short breaks, especially later in the program. A good guitar stand allows you to put it down and pick it right back up again.

12. **Recording Device** – This is optional, and can be as simple as a hand-held digital recorder that you can get for $12 at any department store. Again, simplicity. This is so that you can (optionally) record your practice sessions. This can be a great tool to assess how efficiently and effectively you are practicing and using your time. No need for the DAW here.

Setting up your Workspace

You will need a clean and quiet place to practice where you will not be disturbed. This can be anywhere. The main consideration here is that you can preferably enter your space, sit down, prepare yourself and your materials, and get to work. Having to "set up and tear down" your practice space will make it easier to procrastinate and skip practice. With the materials in the accessories list and some good lighting, you will be all set. Remember this: Your practice space is where you (ideally) will spend many hours of your time. Make it pleasant, accessible, and above all, functional.

Practice

This program requires practice. Consistent and focused practice is necessary to become proficient in any and all facets of guitar playing. In this aspect of your education, it is you who must carry the load and do the work. The bottom line is this: The guitar cannot play itself. There are no short cuts to good technique, and no one can do it for you. It may sound a bit harsh, but it is true. Procrastination has turned many a would-be great guitar player into just an "ok" player, or worse, not a player at all. How do we avoid this? There is a simple answer: make it fun! As long as practicing is fun for you, you'll continue to do it. If you dislike practicing, you won't do it. If you don't do it, you won't improve. If you don't improve, you won't be a guitarist for very long.

In order to develop your guitar playing to its highest level, you must learn to practice slowly...and like it. Many people practice way to fast, but you must practice slowly to develop accuracy. Some guitarists resist the notion of practicing slowly and repetitively because they think it is "boring." However, this is exactly how the brain learns accuracy. Once your brain, muscles, and nerves have developed the proper "memory" to play accurately and efficiently, you will begin to develop the dexterity, strength, and speed that you need and improve all the other aspects of your playing, so that you can play at your best every time.

A good teacher who can help you to see areas of strength and weaknesses is an invaluable asset that can help you to maximize the effectiveness of your practice time. A great teacher will also be able to coach and mentor you as you progress and help you to overcome obstacles as they come up. Your peer groups and other players can help keep you motivated. Listen to great music, see a show, ask questions, get answers, watch a movie, take a walk, do the things you love. Do anything that motivates you, but as the old Nike commercial says: "Just do it!"

Ok, we have our program overview, our materials, our practice space, and our practice pep talk. Now let's get on to some fundamentals.

PART 2 – Fundamentals

Notation, Signs, and Terminology

Preparing to Play – Physical Warm-Up

The Hands – Proper Position and Technique

The Fret Hand

The Picking Hand

Picking Technique

Notation, Tabulature, Signs and Terms

It is not necessary to be able to read music or to know music theory to complete the Daily Burn program. However, a basic understanding of how music is written, particularly the rhythmic element, in addition to guitar tabulature and some common symbols and terminology will be helpful in getting maximum results from the program. The following examples will illustrate these concepts in a very easy to understand format and should be referred back to if you need to clarify something as you work through the program.

The Staff: Measures and Bar lines

All of the notation examples in this book will be written on a staff like the one below. The musical staff is divided into vertical lines called bar lines. The space between two bar lines on a staff is called a measure. Measures divide music into groups of beats. A beat is an equal division of time. A double bar marks the end of a section or example.

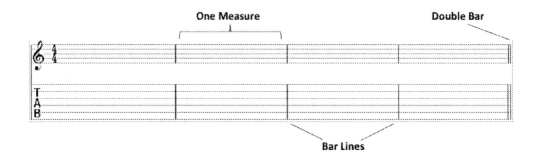

Time Signatures

Every musical staff has two numbers at the beginning called a **time signature**. The top number represents the number of beats in one measure. The bottom number represents the type of note receiving one beat.

Signs and Terms

Here are some useful signs and terms that you will find in this book:

‖: :‖ Repeat.   ⊓ Downstroke.   V Upstroke.

Note Values

In standard notation, the location of a note on the staff indicates its pitch. In this program, you will not need to be concerned with that because all exercises are a repetition of a pattern of finger permutations that will be illustrated in guitar tabulature. However, it is necessary to understand that the duration, or time value, of a note or its corresponding rest is indicated by its shape. The following table is a handy reference:

ITEM	NOTE	REST	VALUE (number of beats)
Whole Note/Rest	o	—	4
Half Note/ Rest	♩	—	2
Quarter Note/Rest	♩	𝄽	1
Eighth Note/Rest	♪	𝄾	1/2
Sixteenth Note/Rest	♬	𝄿	1/4

Guitar Tabulature (TAB)

Tabulature, or "TAB" is an easy to read and effective form of guitar notation. It consists of 6 lines, each one representing a string on the guitar. The top line represents the 1st (high E) string, the bottom line represents the 6th (low E) string. A number placed on the line tells you what fret to play on that string.

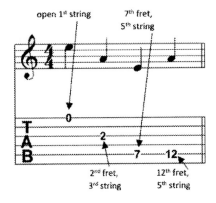

Preparing to Play – Your Physical Daily Warm Up

In order to have effective practices and performances, we must first prepare the body and mind to play. Every good guitar player does it. Just like we wouldn't hop out of bed and run a marathon, we shouldn't expect to come right from another activity, or inactivity, straight into a long practice session, or worse, an important performance. Here are some tips for getting you prepared to play in top form.

Warming up the hands and fingers

You have to physically warm up your hands. Cold hands result in poor performance, muscle strain and fatigue, and many times injuries like tendonitis. Our playing needs to be relaxed and natural, without creating tension. Starting your session with cold hands is a sure way to undermine an otherwise excellent playing experience. There are dozens of simple ways to warm up your hands. Here are a few of my favorites:

1. Rub your hands together until the friction produces heat. Rub the palms and the backs of the hands and fingers.

2. Massage or "knead" each finger and thumb starting at the first knuckle all the way out to the tips. Use the thumb to massage the palm of the opposite hand. Switch hands and repeat.

3. Use all four fingers of the right hand to massage the top of your left forearm. Start near the elbow and work your way down to the wrist. Repeat on the other side.

4. Place your thumb across your opposite wrist. Then, with a very gentle movement, massage the area in a way that is moving across the muscles of the arm. Continue up the arm all the way to the elbow. Switch hands and repeat.

5. Hold your hands overhead and shake them vigorously for about 15 seconds, then let them fall to your side. You'll feel the blood flowing into your hands and fingers. Repeat.

6. Rub your hands under warm water from the faucet (my favorite).

Stretching

Just like any exercise, you always do your best workout if you stretch first. Tight muscles are tired muscles. Too many guitar students wind up cutting good practice short because of fatigue. Here are some good stretches and exercises to get you ready to roll:

1. Hold both hands out in front of you and slowly make a fist, tucking thumbs inside as you exhale. As you inhale, slowly open your fingers out and stretch the fingers apart. Repeat 4 times.

2. Hold your hand out in front of you; make a loose fist with thumbs inside. Holding that hand at the wrist with your other hand, rotate your fist in a complete circle from the wrist. Repeat 4 times clockwise and 4 times counter clockwise. This exercise will open up and loosen the wrist joints and gently stretch and strengthen the muscles responsible for moving the wrist.

3. Hold your palms together in "prayer" fashion with the fingers pointed toward the ceiling. Starting with the index finger, press the left finger into the right so that the right finger stretches back to about a 45 degree angle. Repeat in the opposite direction. Repeat with the middle, ring, and pinky fingers in both directions.

4. Using the thumb and index fingers, gently spread the adjacent fingers of the opposite hands apart. Do this only until you feel a comfortable stretch.

5. Hold your hand out in front in a fist with the thumb pointed toward the ceiling and gently pull the thumb back toward you with the opposite hand. Hold for a few seconds. Repeat on the other hand.

6. Hold your arm out in front of you with your palm facing the floor. Grab your fingertips with the other hand and gently pull them back toward you. Hold for 3 breaths, then release. Repeat on the other side.

7. Do exercise #3, but with the palm turned up and pulling the fingers toward the floor.

8. Clasp the fingers together, turn palms out and push away from you at eye level. Hold 3 breaths, then release.

9. Repeat step 4, but push up and away toward the ceiling. While you're in this position, gently stretch the body to each side laterally, so you feel a nice stretch on the sides of your body.

10. Raise the left arm overhead and bend the elbow, allowing the hand to come down behind your head and between your shoulder blades. Reach up and grab the left elbow with the right hand and gently pull the arm to the right, stretching the left shoulder and upper arm. Repeat on the other side.

11. Look straight ahead and as you exhale, allow your head to tilt to the left, bringing your ear toward your shoulder. Take care not to lift the shoulder to the ear. Hold for 3 breaths. Repeat to the other side.

12. Look straight ahead and as you exhale look up toward the ceiling, stretching the front of the neck. Inhale back to center. Exhale, tuck the chin down and lower the head forward to look at the floor. Inhale to center. Repeat three times.

During your practice sessions, take time every 15 minutes or so to check your position. Holding your instrument with a relaxed posture and good body position is very important. This ensures that you can sustain your practice sessions and make music without tension. It also ensures that you will be able to play for many years without creating the stress and strain on the muscles and joints. Ask yourself: "Is my posture good, or am I hunched over or twisted?", "Am I feeling any tension?", "Am I breathing deeply?" This is important and should never be over looked. The better your posture and playing position, and the more aware you are of tension, the longer and more enjoyable are your practicing and playing sessions, and you will ensure that you are always playing at the top of your game.

This routine should take you about 10-15 minutes. Trust me, it will be the best 10-15 minutes that you can invest in your playing each day. There are many other stretching and warm-up exercises to do. Feel free to experiment. Not only will they get you ready to play, but will help to keep you fit as well.

The Hands – Proper Position and Technique

The correct position of the hands is vitally important to playing the guitar well, and this program is no exception. In fact, proper position of the hands is one of the most important aspects of developing and maintaining good technique and avoiding injury. All of the examples and text in this book, and instructions regarding hand or body positions refer to right-handed players. For left-handed players, simply reverse these instructions

The Left Hand

The left hand should retain a natural and comfortable curve from the forearm, through the wrist and fingers. The thumb should be placed gently on the back of the neck, opposite the middle finger. The wrist should be low and back; you should only touch the guitar with the pad of your thumb and the tips of the fingers. The palm of the hand should not come in contact with the neck. Proper left hand position will allow you to place the fingertips on the strings just behind the frets you are playing. Keep the wrist relaxed and the hand open, and the fingers slightly curled so you will be using leverage rather than pressure to fret the guitar.

Many guitarists make the mistake of applying way too much pressure to fret the notes they are playing. This results in unnecessary tension and strain in the fingers, hands, arms, shoulders, and neck. A great exercise used by many guitarists, to know exactly how much pressure to use, is to just touch the string with the fingertip, muting the note. Begin picking the muted string and gradually begin to press the string just until the note sounds. That is the only pressure you need to sound the note. Any more is just wasted energy. You can even do it without the thumb, putting it in position only after you have the right pressure. Do this exercise often and continue to note how much pressure is necessary. This will create good muscle memory and allow you automatically use the right amount of pressure every time you play.

The Picking Hand

All of the exercises in The Daily Burn are done with a pick. Holding the pick correctly is very important, and is perhaps one of the aspects of technique most commonly overlooked by guitarists. The pick should rest between the pad of your thumb and the left side of the index finger. The tip of the pick should be at a 90-degree angle to the thumb. The index finger is slightly curved so that the pick is resting against the side of the first joint of the finger. The other fingers should hang loosely cupped and relaxed.

The pick should strike the string at a very slight downward angle (nearly 90 degrees). The motion for each pick stroke comes from a combination of the fingers, wrist, hand, and forearm. The wrist should never be rigid, and the motion should never come from the elbow. During picking, the pick should stay close to the strings. Keep the pick strokes short, again only using enough energy to create a full, clean tone. Very lightly bracing the pinky and ring fingers on the top of the guitar for reference can help you to reduce vertical motion (pick moving away from the top of the guitar).

Alternate Picking

There are probably as many ways to pick a guitar as there are guitar players. In this program, we will only concern ourselves with one of them. All of the exercises in The Daily Burn use what is called alternate picking. Alternate picking is exactly what it sounds like. It is the process of playing alternating downstrokes and upstrokes. Alternate picking is one of the best ways to develop synchronization between the right and left hands. This synchronization lies at the very heart of the development of technique, especially the foundation of accuracy, dexterity, strength, and speed, which is the focus of this program.

Alternate picking is very natural, and you should take your time developing it in this program. Remember, The Daily Burn is about *both* hands. When you are playing the exercises in the program, be sure to pay close attention to the picking instructions. It is not difficult, but it is very important.

The basic motion of alternate picking is a combination of the thumb and index finger, the wrist, and the forearm. Many guitarists will place far too much emphasis at the wrist or at the elbow. Both of these create excess tension. If you make sure that you are holding the guitar correctly with your right forearm resting gently on the upper bout of the guitar and the wrist straight, relaxed and without tension, the pick will strike the string at the best angle and you will get the best picking attack. Take care here when planting or bracing the right hand fingers on the guitar as mentioned above. This is just a very light contact, not rigid. Otherwise, it will cause too much movement in the fingers, which can lead to tension. Remember, this bracing of the hand is for reference only. The fingers should curve gently under and glide gently with the pick motion.

Part 3 – The Daily Burn Program

The Daily Burn Program

Welcome to the program. We have all of our fundamentals down. We understand the basics of the left and right hands. We are warmed up. So let's Learn to Burn!!!

This program is designed to be done daily, at the beginning of your practice, and followed exactly as instructed and in the order given. Remember that it is a tried and true system used by many guitarists and teachers for many years. There's no need to fix what isn't broken.

There's no need to skip around or try to move through it quicker than a day at a time. This is how it does its work, slowly and methodically. Remember, that in many cases we are learning, re-learning, or un-learning certain habitual movement patterns. Let the program do its work, and it *will work.*

Daily Practice Logs and Tracking Your Progress

There is no better way to practice anything on the guitar than to keep a written log of your progress. That's because it is a constant positive feedback. The practice log is a constant reminder of the progress you are making. It's all there in black and white. Tracking your progress is vital to your success in this program and as a guitarist.

The Daily Burn program is written as a practice routine, practice log, and progress tracking system all in one. That is why it is so successful and has been for so many students. As you move through the routine each day, you'll record your results in the spaces provided (use pencil). These results will set the stage for the following day's practice. Each day, you will improve, and your daily routine will be based on the previous day's results. It's that simple, really. Just follow the program each day and you will be playing (or back to playing) at the top of your game in no time. And better yet, you'll stay that way.

Guitar Speed Development

In this program, we will use a very specific method for developing accuracy, dexterity, strength and speed using a metronome. Here is an overview of how it's done:

1. Gather your materials and set up your practice space.

2. Make sure that your hands, fingers and body are warmed up properly.

3. For all exercises, you will begin by playing eighth notes at a speed of 40 bpm on the metronome.

4. Play each exercise in the "marker position", that is, positions 1, 3, 5, 7, 9, and 12.

5. With each new exercise, you will first find the maximum speed at which you can play the exercise accurately, with all notes sounding clean and even. No tension.

6. After beginning at 40 bpm (which is the lowest setting on the metronome, and very slow), you will continue to increase the speed at every position by 6 bpm on the metronome (i.e. position 1 @ 40, position 3 @ 46, position 5 @ 52, etc.) until you reach maximum clean speed.

7. Write this speed down in the space provided in that day's log. This is max speed #1. Write in your time.

8. Practice the technique at 30% of your max speed. Practice at this speed each day for 5 practice sessions, for the specified length of time. Don't concern yourself with trying to play faster. Everything must be clean, with no tension. Be patient, so that you avoid training your hands to play poorly. You are developing muscle memory (and remember...muscles remember how to do something incorrectly just as easily as they can remember how to do it correctly.

9. Practice at 50% of max speed #1 for 3 practice sessions.

10. Practice at 65% of max speed #1 for 3 practice sessions.

11. Re-evaluate max speed, starting at your 65% speed. This is max speed #2. Log your time.

12. Practice at 80% of max speed #2 for 5 consecutive sessions.

13. Re-evaluate max speed, starting at your 80% speed. This is max speed #3. Log your time.

14. Practice at 90% of max speed #3 for 5 practice sessions.

15. Re-evaluate max speed, starting at your 90% speed. This is max speed #4. Log your time.

Once you have reached this point, max speed #4, you are at a maintenance level for the exercise. You can continue to do the exercise as needed. Blank practice logs are included at the back of the book, for you to make copies of and record your progress. Simply follow these instructions:

1. Rotate 2 sessions each @ 60%, 85%, and 95%. Use the same specs as above.

2. Once a week, measure your new max speed and adjust the metronome accordingly.
    Repeat.

Finger Permutations

The Daily Burn program is based entirely on practicing different combinations of 60 permutations of the fingers of the left (fretting) hand, in a specific order, for a specific length of time, and at a specific speed. All exercises will utilize alternate picking. You should follow the program exactly as it is written. It is designed in such a way that these combinations will work to develop the nervous system and muscular movement patterns to become more efficient and balanced. This is very important, because it is this balance that allows you to develop and maintain your accuracy, dexterity, strength and speed at optimal levels.

There are three basic groups of permutations: 2-finger groups, 3-finger groups, and 4-finger groups. These groups are further broken down into smaller groups that focus on specific muscular movements. The following tables illustrate all of the groups of permutations used in The Daily Burn Program.

2-finger	3-finger	4-finger
1-2/2-1	1-2-3 / 2-3-4 3-4-1 / 4-1-2	1-2-3-4 / 2-3-4-1 3-4-1-2 / 4-1-2-3
1-3/3-1	1-2-4 / 2-4-3 4-3-1 / 3-1-2	1-2-4-3 /2-4-3-1 4-3-1-2 / 3-1-2-4
1-4/4-1	1-3-2 / 3-2-4 2-4-1 / 4-1-3	1-3-2-4 / 3-2-4-1 2-4-1-3 / 4-1-3-2
2-3/3-2	1-3-4 / 3-4-2 4-2-1 / 2-1-3	1-3-4-2 / 3-4-2-1 4-2-1-3 / 2-1-3-4
2-4/4-2	1-4-2 / 4-2-3 2-3-1 / 3-1-4	1-4-2-3 / 4-2-3-1 2-3-1-4 / 3-1-4-2
3-4/4-3	1-4-3 / 4-3-2 3-2-1 / 2-1-4	1-4-3-2 / 4-3-2-1 3-2-1-4 / 2-1-4-3

Finger Permutation Exercises Overview

All of the permutation exercises in the program are located right here in one place so that you may have an easy to use and convenient point of reference. All exercises are shown in standard notation and TAB, and all notation is written in position 1. For example: 1-2-3-4 on the TAB staff indicates that you would play frets 1, 2, 3, and 4 in that order on a given string. However, that same permutation will be played on each string, ascending and descending in different positions up and down the neck. In other words, in each exercise the TAB notation also specifies the permutation. In the program's daily log pages, you will see each exercise listed as a permutation. For example: "1-2-3-4" refers to that specific permutation, regardless of the position you are playing in. Look them over and try them out, but don't be concerned with learning all of them right now. Once you begin the daily practices, refer back here to see the permutation and begin working on your routine.

Permutation Exercises

In the 2-finger permutations, you will play one pattern ascending and the opposite pattern descending (i.e. 1-2 ascending, 2-1 descending). For 3 and 4-finger permutations, use the same pattern ascending and descending. All exercises use alternate picking throughout. Pay special attention to the ascending and descending picking patterns.

2-finger permutations: Ascending Picking Pattern ⊓ V ⊓ V / Descending Picking Pattern V ⊓ V ⊓

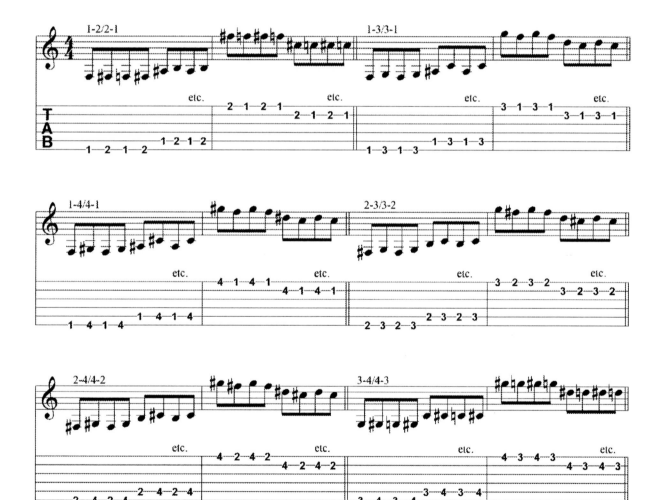

3-finger permutations: Ascending Picking Pattern ⊓ V ⊓ V / Descending Picking Pattern V ⊓ V ⊓

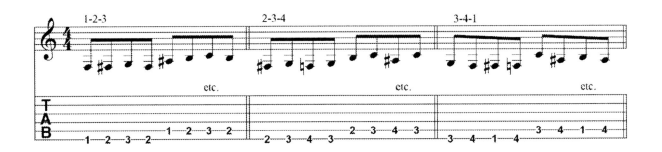

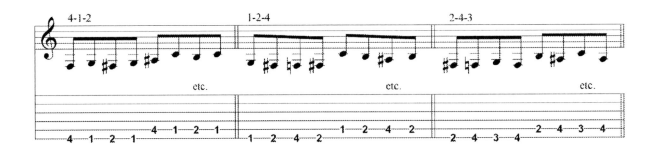

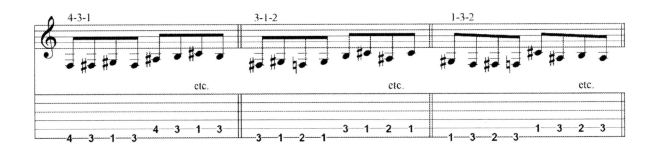

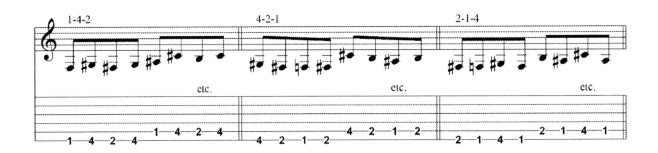

4-finger permutations: Ascending Picking Pattern ⊓ V ⊓ V / Descending Picking Pattern V ⊓ V ⊓

The Daily Practices

Instructions

All you need to do now is to practice. Simply start at day 1 and work your way through the program, following it in order. Refer to the exercise section for the TAB, notation, and picking instructions for each permutation exercise. Here are a few suggestions to help you maximize your daily practice:

1. Don't try to learn all the exercise before you start. Just begin with Day 1. You can refer to the proper exercise by its name (i.e. "1-2/2-1" or "1-4-2-3") in the log. Then simply come back to the exercise section, go through the correct exercise to make sure you have it, and start in on that day's program.

2. Begin each day's routine with the exercise that has the slowest starting speed. This will ensure that your hands are prepared for the faster speeds to follow. Remember that finding all max speed #1 sessions start at 40 bpm. It is also a good idea to start the exercises at lower speeds for a few repetitions to get your fingers accustomed to the permutation before moving to your program day speeds.

3. Each day's program will take about 30 minutes (a great amount of time to practice technique, by the way!!!) Plan extra time on the days when you are finding "max speeds", as these take longer than the daily drills that work at specific speeds for shorter lengths of time.

4. If you don't have time to do the daily routine all at once, break it up into smaller sessions. Just make sure that before each session that you do the physical warm-up. This is important!!!

5. Take breaks. Every 10 minutes or so, put the guitar down for a minute. Stand up, stretch.

6. Be sure to date each day's log and fill it in every day. Also, it may help you to figure out the next day's metronome settings at the end of your practice and place them in the next day's log, so that you are ready to go the next day. This will eliminate having to flip back through the book.

7. Once you reach a maintenance level for a given exercise, it will appear in that day's chart as "maintenance level" on the first day. After that, it will drop off the chart and you should work on it as needed. There are templates at the back of the book for you to photocopy and use for maintenance work.

8. You should continue to do maintenance work, or at the very least use some of the simple permutations as slow warm-ups. This holds especially true towards the end of the program when the speeds are all quite fast.

9. Be patient. This is a program that builds slowly and methodically. Simply do the program, rest, and move on to your other musical projects. Let the program work.

All exercises should begin by playing eighth notes (two notes per beat) on the metronome. If you have worked your way up to 208 bpm (the highest metronome setting), continue by playing each exercise in sixteenth notes (four notes per beat), starting at 104 bpm. When practicing the permutations, play them at each "marker position" (positions 1, 3, 5, 7, 9, and 12) up and down the neck. This method gives you a great cross-section of the various sizes of the positions on the neck. It is also convenient to move from "dot-to dot" on the fingerboard rather than one position at a time (which can get a bit tedious).

Take your time, enjoy the process,
and prepare to see great results. Have fun!!!

DAY 1	Date __ /__ /____	
EXERCISE PERMUTATION ASCENDING/DESCENDING	EXERCISE DETAIL and METRONOME SPEED SETTING	TIME
1-2/2-1	Max Speed 1: _____	

DAY 2	Date __ /__ /____	
EXERCISE PERMUTATION ASCENDING/DESCENDING	EXERCISE DETAIL and METRONOME SPEED SETTING	TIME
1-3/3-1	Max Speed 1: _____	
1-2/2-1	Day 1 @ 30% Max Speed 1: _____	3m

DAY 3	Date __ /__ /____	
EXERCISE PERMUTATION ASCENDING/DESCENDING	EXERCISE DETAIL and METRONOME SPEED SETTING	TIME
1-4/4-1	Max Speed 1: _____	
1-3/3-1	Day 1 @ 30% Max Speed 1: _____	3m
1-2/2-1	Day 2 @ 30% Max Speed 1: _____	3m

DAY 4	Date __ /__ /____	
EXERCISE PERMUTATION ASCENDING/DESCENDING	EXERCISE DETAIL and METRONOME SPEED SETTING	TIME
2-3/3-2	Max Speed 1: _____	
1-4/4-1	Day 1 @ 30% Max Speed 1: _____	3m
1-3/3-1	Day 2 @ 30% Max Speed 1: _____	3m
1-2/2-1	Day 3 @ 30% Max Speed 1: _____	3m

DAY 5	Date __ / __ / ____	
EXERCISE PERMUTATION ASCENDING/DESCENDING	EXERCISE DETAIL and METRONOME SPEED SETTING	TIME
2-4/4-2	Max Speed 1: _____	
2-3/3-2	Day 1 @ 30% Max Speed 1: _____	3m
1-4/4-1	Day 2 @ 30% Max Speed 1: _____	3m
1-3/3-1	Day 3 @ 30% Max Speed 1: _____	3m
1-2/2-1	Day 4 @ 30% Max Speed 1: _____	3m

DAY 6	Date __ / __ / ____	
EXERCISE PERMUTATION ASCENDING/DESCENDING	EXERCISE DETAIL and METRONOME SPEED SETTING	TIME
3-4/4-3	Max Speed 1: _____	
2-4/4-2	Day 1 @ 30% Max Speed 1: _____	3m
2-3/3-2	Day 2 @ 30% Max Speed 1: _____	3m
1-4/4-1	Day 3 @ 30% Max Speed 1: _____	3m
1-3/3-1	Day 4 @ 30% Max Speed 1: _____	3m
1-2/2-1	Day 5 @ 30% Max Speed 1: _____	3m

DAY 7	Date __ / __ / ____	
EXERCISE PERMUTATION ASCENDING/DESCENDING	EXERCISE DETAIL and METRONOME SPEED SETTING	TIME
3-4/4-3	Day 1 @ 30% Max Speed 1: _____	3m
2-4/4-2	Day 2 @ 30% Max Speed 1: _____	3m
2-3/3-2	Day 3 @ 30% Max Speed 1: _____	3m
1-4/4-1	Day 4 @ 30% Max Speed 1: _____	3m
1-3/3-1	Day 5 @ 30% Max Speed 1: _____	3m
1-2/2-1	Day 1 @ 50% Max Speed 1: _____	3m

DAY 8	Date __ /__ /____	
EXERCISE PERMUTATION ASCENDING/DESCENDING	EXERCISE DETAIL and METRONOME SPEED SETTING	TIME
3-4/4-3	Day 2 @ 30% Max Speed 1: _____	3m
2-4/4-2	Day 3 @ 30% Max Speed 1: _____	3m
2-3/3-2	Day 4 @ 30% Max Speed 1: _____	3m
1-4/4-1	Day 5 @ 30% Max Speed 1: _____	3m
1-3/3-1	Day 1 @ 50% Max Speed 1: _____	3m
1-2/2-1	Day 2 @ 50% Max Speed 1: _____	3m

DAY 9	Date __ /__ /____	
EXERCISE PERMUTATION ASCENDING/DESCENDING	EXERCISE DETAIL and METRONOME SPEED SETTING	TIME
3-4/4-3	Day 3 @ 30% Max Speed 1: _____	3m
2-4/4-2	Day 4 @ 30% Max Speed 1: _____	3m
2-3/3-2	Day 5 @ 30% Max Speed 1: _____	3m
1-4/4-1	Day 1 @ 50% Max Speed 1: _____	3m
1-3/3-1	Day 2 @ 50% Max Speed 1: _____	3m
1-2/2-1	Day 3 @ 50% Max Speed 1: _____	3m

DAY 10	Date __ /__ /____	
EXERCISE PERMUTATION ASCENDING/DESCENDING	EXERCISE DETAIL and METRONOME SPEED SETTING	TIME
3-4/4-3	Day 4 @ 30% Max Speed 1: _____	3m
2-4/4-2	Day 5 @ 30% Max Speed 1: _____	3m
2-3/3-2	Day 1 @ 50% Max Speed 1: _____	3m
1-4/4-1	Day 2 @ 50% Max Speed 1: _____	3m
1-3/3-1	Day 3 @ 50% Max Speed 1: _____	3m
1-2/2-1	Day 1 @ 65% Max Speed 1: _____	3m

DAY 11	Date __ / __ / ____	
EXERCISE PERMUTATION ASCENDING/DESCENDING	EXERCISE DETAIL and METRONOME SPEED SETTING	TIME
3-4/4-3	Day 5 @ 30% Max Speed 1: _____	3m
2-4/4-2	Day 1 @ 50% Max Speed 1: _____	3m
2-3/3-2	Day 2 @ 50% Max Speed 1: _____	3m
1-4/4-1	Day 3 @ 50% Max Speed 1: _____	3m
1-3/3-1	Day 1 @ 65% Max Speed 1: _____	3m
1-2/2-1	Day 2 @ 65% Max Speed 1: _____	3m

DAY 12	Date __ / __ / ____	
EXERCISE PERMUTATION ASCENDING/DESCENDING	EXERCISE DETAIL and METRONOME SPEED SETTING	TIME
3-4/4-3	Day 1 @ 50% Max Speed 1: _____	3m
2-4/4-2	Day 2 @ 50% Max Speed 1: _____	3m
2-3/3-2	Day 3 @ 50% Max Speed 1: _____	3m
1-4/4-1	Day 1 @ 65% Max Speed 1: _____	3m
1-3/3-1	Day 2 @ 65% Max Speed 1: _____	3m
1-2/2-1	Day 2 @ 65% Max Speed 1: _____	3m

DAY 13	Date __ / __ / ____	
EXERCISE PERMUTATION ASCENDING/DESCENDING	EXERCISE DETAIL and METRONOME SPEED SETTING	TIME
3-4/4-3	Day 2 @ 50% Max Speed 1: _____	3m
2-4/4-2	Day 3 @ 50% Max Speed 1: _____	3m
2-3/3-2	Day 1 @ 65% Max Speed 1: _____	3m
1-4/4-1	Day 2 @ 65% Max Speed 1: _____	3m
1-3/3-1	Day 3 @ 65% Max Speed 1: _____	3m
1-2/2-1	Max Speed 2: _____	

DAY 14	Date __ / __ / ____	
EXERCISE PERMUTATION ASCENDING/DESCENDING	EXERCISE DETAIL and METRONOME SPEED SETTING	TIME
1-2-3	Max speed 1: _____	
3-4/4-3	Day 3 @ 50% Max Speed 1: _____	3m
2-4/4-2	Day 1 @ 65% Max Speed 1: _____	3m
2-3/3-2	Day 2 @ 65% Max Speed 1: _____	3m
1-4/4-1	Day 3 @ 65% Max Speed 1: _____	3m
1-3/3-1	Max Speed 2: _____	
1-2/2-1	Day 1 @ 80% Max Speed 2: _____	3m

DAY 15	Date __ / __ / ____	
EXERCISE PERMUTATION ASCENDING/DESCENDING	EXERCISE DETAIL and METRONOME SPEED SETTING	TIME
1-2-3	Day 1 @ 30% Max speed 1: _____	3m
3-4/4-3	Day 1 @ 65% Max Speed 1: _____	3m
2-4/4-2	Day 2 @ 65% Max Speed 1: _____	3m
2-3/3-2	Day 3 @ 65% Max Speed 1: _____	3m
1-4/4-1	Max Speed 2: _____	
1-3/3-1	Day 1 @ 80% Max Speed 2: _____	3m
1-2/2-1	Day 2 @ 80% Max Speed 2: _____	3m

DAY 16	Date __ / __ / ____	
EXERCISE PERMUTATION ASCENDING/DESCENDING	EXERCISE DETAIL and METRONOME SPEED SETTING	TIME
1-2-3	Day 2 @ 30% Max speed 1: _____	3m
3-4/4-3	Day 2 @ 65% Max Speed 1: _____	3m
2-4/4-2	Day 3 @ 65% Max Speed 1: _____	3m
2-3/3-2	Max Speed 2: _____	
1-4/4-1	Day 1 @ 80% Max Speed 2: _____	3m
1-3/3-1	Day 2 @ 80% Max Speed 2: _____	3m
1-2/2-1	Day 3 @ 80% Max Speed 2: _____	3m

DAY 17	Date __ / __ / ____	
EXERCISE PERMUTATION ASCENDING/DESCENDING	EXERCISE DETAIL and METRONOME SPEED SETTING	TIME
1-2-3	Day 3 @ 30% Max speed 1: _____	3m
3-4/4-3	Day 3 @ 65% Max Speed 1: _____	3m
2-4/4-2	Max Speed 2: _____	
2-3/3-2	Day 1 @ 80% Max Speed 2: _____	3m
1-4/4-1	Day 2 @ 80% Max Speed 2: _____	3m
1-3/3-1	Day 3 @ 80% Max Speed 2: _____	3m
1-2/2-1	Day 4 @ 80% Max Speed 2: _____	3m

DAY 18	Date __ / __ / ____	
EXERCISE PERMUTATION ASCENDING/DESCENDING	EXERCISE DETAIL and METRONOME SPEED SETTING	TIME
1-2-3	Day 4 @ 30% Max speed 1: _____	3m
3-4/4-3	Max Speed 2: _____	
2-4/4-2	Day 1 @ 80% Max Speed 2: _____	3m
2-3/3-2	Day 2 @ 80% Max Speed 2: _____	3m
1-4/4-1	Day 3 @ 80% Max Speed 2: _____	3m
1-3/3-1	Day 4 @ 80% Max Speed 2: _____	3m
1-2/2-1	Day 5 @ 80% Max Speed 2: _____	3m

DAY 19	Date __ / __ / ____	
EXERCISE PERMUTATION ASCENDING/DESCENDING	EXERCISE DETAIL and METRONOME SPEED SETTING	TIME
1-2-3	Day 5 @ 30% Max Speed 1: _____	3m
3-4/4-3	Day 1 @ 80% Max Speed 2: _____	3m
2-4/4-2	Day 2 @ 80% Max Speed 2: _____	3m
2-3/3-2	Day 3 @ 80% Max Speed 2: _____	3m
1-4/4-1	Day 4 @ 80% Max Speed 2: _____	3m
1-3/3-1	Day 5 @ 80% Max Speed 2: _____	3m
1-2/2-1	Max Speed 3: _____	

DAY 20	Date __ / __ / ____	
EXERCISE PERMUTATION ASCENDING/DESCENDING	EXERCISE DETAIL and METRONOME SPEED SETTING	TIME
1-2-3	Day 1 @ 50% Max Speed 1: _____	3m
3-4/4-3	Day 2 @ 80% Max Speed 2: _____	3m
2-4/4-2	Day 3 @ 80% Max Speed 2: _____	3m
2-3/3-2	Day 4 @ 80% Max Speed 2: _____	3m
1-4/4-1	Day 5 @ 80% Max Speed 2: _____	3m
1-3/3-1	Max Speed 3: _____	
1-2/2-1	Day 1 @ 90%Max Speed 3: _____	3m

DAY 21	Date __ / __ / ____	
EXERCISE PERMUTATION ASCENDING/DESCENDING	EXERCISE DETAIL and METRONOME SPEED SETTING	TIME
1-2-3	Day 2 @ 50% Max Speed 1: _____	3m
3-4/4-3	Day 3 @ 80% Max Speed 2: _____	3m
2-4/4-2	Day 4 @ 80% Max Speed 2: _____	3m
2-3/3-2	Day 5 @ 80% Max Speed 2: _____	3m
1-4/4-1	Max Speed 3: _____	
1-3/3-1	Day 1 @ 90% Max Speed 3: _____	3m
1-2/2-1	Day 2 @ 90% Max Speed 3: _____	3m

DAY 22	Date __ / __ / ____	
EXERCISE PERMUTATION ASCENDING/DESCENDING	EXERCISE DETAIL and METRONOME SPEED SETTING	TIME
1-2-3	Day 3 @ 50% Max Speed 1: _____	3m
3-4/4-3	Day 4 @ 80% Max Speed 2: _____	3m
2-4/4-2	Day 5 @ 80% Max Speed 2: _____	3m
2-3/3-2	Max Speed 3: _____	3m
1-4/4-1	Day 1 @ 90% Max Speed 3: _____	
1-3/3-1	Day 2 @ 90% Max Speed 3: _____	3m
1-2/2-1	Day 3 @ 90%Max Speed 3: _____	3m

DAY 23	Date __ / __ / ____	
EXERCISE PERMUTATION ASCENDING/DESCENDING	EXERCISE DETAIL and METRONOME SPEED SETTING	TIME
2-3-4	Max Speed 1: _____	
1-2-3	Day 1 @ 65% Max Speed 1: _____	3m
3-4/4-3	Day 5 @ 80% Max Speed 2: _____	3m
2-4/4-2	Max Speed 3: _____	
2-3/3-2	Day 1 @ 90% Max Speed 3: _____	3m
1-4/4-1	Day 2 @ 90% Max Speed 3: _____	3m
1-3/3-1	Day 3 @ 90% Max Speed 3: _____	3m
1-2/2-1	Day 4 @ 90% Max Speed 3: _____	3m

DAY 24	Date __ / __ / ____	
EXERCISE PERMUTATION ASCENDING/DESCENDING	EXERCISE DETAIL and METRONOME SPEED SETTING	TIME
2-3-4	Day 1 @ 30% Max Speed 1: _____	3m
1-2-3	Day 2 @ 65% Max Speed 1: _____	3m
3-4/4-3	Max Speed 3: _____	
2-4/4-2	Day 1 @ 90% Max Speed 3: _____	3m
2-3/3-2	Day 2 @ 90% Max Speed 3: _____	3m
1-4/4-1	Day 3 @ 90% Max Speed 3: _____	3m
1-3/3-1	Day 4 @ 90% Max Speed 3: _____	3m
1-2/2-1	Day 5 @ 90% Max Speed 3: _____	3m

DAY 25	Date __ / __ / ____	
EXERCISE PERMUTATION ASCENDING/DESCENDING	EXERCISE DETAIL and METRONOME SPEED SETTING	TIME
2-3-4	Day 2 @ 30% Max Speed 1: _____	3m
1-2-3	Day 3 @ 65% Max Speed 1: _____	3m
3-4/4-3	Day 1 @ 90% Max Speed 3: _____	3m
2-4/4-2	Day 2 @ 90% Max Speed 3: _____	3m
2-3/3-2	Day 3 @ 90% Max Speed 3: _____	3m
1-4/4-1	Day 4 @ 90% Max Speed 3: _____	3m
1-3/3-1	Day 5 @ 90% Max Speed 3: _____	3m
1-2/2-1	Max Speed 4: _____ Maintenance Level	

DAY 26	Date __ / __ / ____	
EXERCISE PERMUTATION ASCENDING/DESCENDING	EXERCISE DETAIL and METRONOME SPEED SETTING	TIME
2-3-4	Day 3 @ 30% Max Speed 1: _____	3m
1-2-3	Max Speed 2: _____	
3-4/4-3	Day 2 @ 90% Max Speed 3: _____	3m
2-4/4-2	Day 3 @ 90% Max Speed 3: _____	3m
2-3/3-2	Day 4 @ 90% Max Speed 3: _____	3m
1-4/4-1	Day 5 @ 90% Max Speed 3: _____	3m
1-3/3-1	Max Speed 4: _____ Maintenance Level	3m

DAY 27	Date __ / __ / ____	
EXERCISE PERMUTATION ASCENDING/DESCENDING	EXERCISE DETAIL and METRONOME SPEED SETTING	TIME
3-4-1	Max Speed 1: _____	
2-3-4	Day 4 @ 30% Max Speed 1: _____	3m
1-2-3	Day 1 @ 80% Max Speed 2: _____	3m
3-4/4-3	Day 3 @ 90% Max Speed 3: _____	3m
2-4/4-2	Day 4 @ 90% Max Speed 3: _____	3m
2-3/3-2	Day 5 @ 90% Max Speed 3: _____	3m
1-4/4-1	Max Speed 4: _____ Maintenance Level	

DAY 28	Date __ / __ / ____	
EXERCISE PERMUTATION ASCENDING/DESCENDING	EXERCISE DETAIL and METRONOME SPEED SETTING	TIME
4-1-2	Max Speed 1: _____	
3-4-1	Day 1 @ 30% Max Speed 1: _____	3m
2-3-4	Day 5 @ 30% Max Speed 1: _____	3m
1-2-3	Day 2 @ 80% Max Speed 2: _____	3m
3-4/4-3	Day 4 @ 90% Max Speed 3: _____	3m
2-4/4-2	Day 5 @ 90% Max Speed 3: _____	3m
2-3/3-2	Max Speed 4: _____ Maintenance Level	

DAY 29	Date __ / __ / ____	
EXERCISE PERMUTATION ASCENDING/DESCENDING	EXERCISE DETAIL and METRONOME SPEED SETTING	TIME
1-2-4	Max Speed 1: _____	
4-1-2	Day 1 @ 30% Max Speed 1: _____	3m
3-4-1	Day 2 @ 30% Max Speed 1: _____	3m
2-3-4	Day 1 @ 50% Max Speed 1: _____	3m
1-2-3	Day 3 @ 80% Max Speed 2: _____	3m
3-4/4-3	Day 5 @ 90% Max Speed 3: _____	3m
2-4/4-2	Max Speed 4: _____ Maintenance Level	

DAY 30	Date __ / __ / ____	
EXERCISE PERMUTATION ASCENDING/DESCENDING	EXERCISE DETAIL and METRONOME SPEED SETTING	TIME
2-4-3	Max Speed 1: _____	
1-2-4	Day 1 @ 30% Max Speed 1: _____	3m
4-1-2	Day 2 @ 30% Max Speed 1: _____	3m
3-4-1	Day 3 @ 30% Max Speed 1: _____	3m
2-3-4	Day 2 @ 50% Max Speed 1: _____	3m
1-2-3	Day 4 @ 80% Max Speed 2: _____	3m
3-4/4-3	Max Speed 4: _____ Maintenance Level	

DAY 31	Date __ / __ / ____	
EXERCISE PERMUTATION ASCENDING/DESCENDING	EXERCISE DETAIL and METRONOME SPEED SETTING	TIME
4-3-1	Max Speed 1: _____	
2-4-3	Day 1 @ 30% Max Speed 1: _____	3m
1-2-4	Day 2 @ 30% Max Speed 1: _____	3m
4-1-2	Day 3 @ 30% Max Speed 1: _____	3m
3-4-1	Day 4 @ 30% Max Speed 1: _____	3m
2-3-4	Day 3 @ 50% Max Speed 1: _____	3m
1-2-3	Day 5 @ 80% Max Speed 2: _____	3m

DAY 32	Date __ / __ / ____	
EXERCISE PERMUTATION ASCENDING/DESCENDING	EXERCISE DETAIL and METRONOME SPEED SETTING	TIME
4-3-1	Day 1 @ 30% Max Speed 1: _____	3m
2-4-3	Day 2 @ 30% Max Speed 1: _____	3m
1-2-4	Day 3 @ 30% Max Speed 1: _____	3m
4-1-2	Day 4 @ 30% Max Speed 1: _____	3m
3-4-1	Day 5 @ 30% Max Speed 1: _____	3m
2-3-4	Day 1 @ 65% Max Speed 1: _____	3m
1-2-3	Max Speed 3: _____	

DAY 33	Date __ / __ / ____	
EXERCISE PERMUTATION ASCENDING/DESCENDING	EXERCISE DETAIL and METRONOME SPEED SETTING	TIME
4-3-1	Day 2 @ 30% Max Speed 1: _____	3m
2-4-3	Day 3 @ 30% Max Speed 1: _____	3m
1-2-4	Day 4 @ 30% Max Speed 1: _____	3m
4-1-2	Day 5 @ 30% Max Speed 1: _____	3m
3-4-1	Day 1 @ 50% Max Speed 1: _____	3m
2-3-4	Day 2 @ 65% Max Speed 1: _____	3m
1-2-3	Day 1 @ 90% Max Speed 3: _____	3m

DAY 34	Date __ / __ / ____	
EXERCISE PERMUTATION ASCENDING/DESCENDING	EXERCISE DETAIL and METRONOME SPEED SETTING	TIME
4-3-1	Day 3 @ 30% Max Speed 1: _____	3m
2-4-3	Day 4 @ 30% Max Speed 1: _____	3m
1-2-4	Day 5 @ 30% Max Speed 1: _____	3m
4-1-2	Day 1 @ 50% Max Speed 1: _____	3m
3-4-1	Day 2 @ 50% Max Speed 1: _____	3m
2-3-4	Day 3 @ 65% Max Speed 1: _____	3m
1-2-3	Day 2 @ 90% Max Speed 3: _____	3m

DAY 35	Date __ / __ / ____	
EXERCISE PERMUTATION ASCENDING/DESCENDING	EXERCISE DETAIL and METRONOME SPEED SETTING	TIME
4-3-1	Day 4 @ 30% Max Speed 1: _____	3m
2-4-3	Day 5 @ 30% Max Speed 1: _____	3m
1-2-4	Day 1 @ 50% Max Speed 1: _____	3m
4-1-2	Day 2 @ 50% Max Speed 1: _____	3m
3-4-1	Day 3 @ 50% Max Speed 1: _____	3m
2-3-4	Max Speed 2: _____	
1-2-3	Day 2 @ 90% Max Speed 3: _____	3m

DAY 36	Date __ / __ / ____	
EXERCISE PERMUTATION ASCENDING/DESCENDING	EXERCISE DETAIL and METRONOME SPEED SETTING	TIME
4-3-1	Day 5 @ 30% Max Speed 1: _____	3m
2-4-3	Day 1 @ 50% Max Speed 1: _____	3m
1-2-4	Day 2 @ 50% Max Speed 1: _____	3m
4-1-2	Day 3 @ 50% Max Speed 1: _____	3m
3-4-1	Day 1 @ 65% Max Speed 1: _____	3m
2-3-4	Day 1 @ 80% Max Speed 2: _____	3m
1-2-3	Day 3 @ 90% Max Speed 3: _____	3m

DAY 37	Date __ / __ / ____	
EXERCISE PERMUTATION ASCENDING/DESCENDING	EXERCISE DETAIL and METRONOME SPEED SETTING	TIME
4-3-1	Day 1 @ 50% Max Speed 1: _____	3m
2-4-3	Day 2 @ 50% Max Speed 1: _____	3m
1-2-4	Day 3 @ 50% Max Speed 1: _____	3m
4-1-2	Day 1 @ 65% Max Speed 1: _____	3m
3-4-1	Day 2 @ 65% Max Speed 1: _____	3m
2-3-4	Day 2 @ 80% Max Speed 2: _____	3m
1-2-3	Day 4 @ 90% Max Speed 3: _____	3m

DAY 38	Date __ / __ / ____	
EXERCISE PERMUTATION ASCENDING/DESCENDING	EXERCISE DETAIL and METRONOME SPEED SETTING	TIME
4-3-1	Day 2 @ 50% Max Speed 1: _____	3m
2-4-3	Day 3 @ 50% Max Speed 1: _____	3m
1-2-4	Day 1 @ 65% Max Speed 1: _____	3m
4-1-2	Day 2 @ 65% Max Speed 1: _____	3m
3-4-1	Day 3 @ 65% Max Speed 1: _____	3m
2-3-4	Day 3 @ 80% Max Speed 2: _____	3m
1-2-3	Day 5 @ 90% Max Speed 3: _____	3m

DAY 39	Date __ / __ / ____	
EXERCISE PERMUTATION ASCENDING/DESCENDING	EXERCISE DETAIL and METRONOME SPEED SETTING	TIME
4-3-1	Day 3 @ 50% Max Speed 1: _____	3m
2-4-3	Day 1 @ 65% Max Speed 1: _____	3m
1-2-4	Day 2 @ 65% Max Speed 1: _____	3m
4-1-2	Day 3 @ 65% Max Speed 1: _____	3m
3-4-1	Max Speed 2: _____	
2-3-4	Day 4 @ 80% Max Speed 2: _____	3m
1-2-3	Max Speed 4: _____ Maintenance Level	

DAY 40	Date __ / __ / ____	
EXERCISE PERMUTATION ASCENDING/DESCENDING	EXERCISE DETAIL and METRONOME SPEED SETTING	TIME
3-1-2	Max Speed 1: _____	
4-3-1	Day 1 @ 65% Max Speed 1: _____	3m
2-4-3	Day 2 @ 65% Max Speed 1: _____	3m
1-2-4	Day 3 @ 65% Max Speed 1: _____	3m
4-1-2	Max Speed 2: _____	
3-4-1	Day 1 @ 80% Max Speed 2: _____	3m
2-3-4	Day 5 @ 80% Max Speed 2: _____	3m

DAY 41	Date __ / __ / ____	
EXERCISE PERMUTATION ASCENDING/DESCENDING	EXERCISE DETAIL and METRONOME SPEED SETTING	TIME
3-1-2	Day 1 @ 30% Max Speed 1: _____	3m
4-3-1	Day 2 @ 65% Max Speed 1: _____	3m
2-4-3	Day 3 @ 65% Max Speed 1: _____	3m
1-2-4	Max Speed 2: _____	
4-1-2	Day 1 @ 80% Max Speed 2: _____	3m
3-4-1	Day 2 @ 80% Max Speed 2: _____	3m
2-3-4	Max Speed 3: _____	

DAY 42	Date __ / __ / ____	
EXERCISE PERMUTATION ASCENDING/DESCENDING	EXERCISE DETAIL and METRONOME SPEED SETTING	TIME
3-1-2	Day 2 @ 30% Max Speed 1: _____	3m
4-3-1	Day 3 @ 65% Max Speed 1: _____	3m
2-4-3	Max Speed 2: _____	
1-2-4	Day 1 @ 80% Max Speed 2: _____	3m
4-1-2	Day 2 @ 80% Max Speed 2: _____	3m
3-4-1	Day 3 @ 80% Max Speed 2: _____	3m
2-3-4	Day 1 @ 90% Max Speed 3: _____	3m

DAY 43	Date __ / __ / ____	
EXERCISE PERMUTATION ASCENDING/DESCENDING	EXERCISE DETAIL and METRONOME SPEED SETTING	TIME
3-1-2	Day 3 @ 30% Max Speed 1: _____	3m
4-3-1	Max Speed 2: _____	
2-4-3	Day 1 @ 80% Max Speed 2: _____	3m
1-2-4	Day 2 @ 80% Max Speed 2: _____	3m
4-1-2	Day 3 @ 80% Max Speed 2: _____	3m
3-4-1	Day 4 @ 80% Max Speed 2: _____	3m
2-3-4	Day 2 @ 90% Max Speed 3: _____	3m

DAY 44	Date __ / __ / ____	
EXERCISE PERMUTATION ASCENDING/DESCENDING	EXERCISE DETAIL and METRONOME SPEED SETTING	TIME
3-1-2	Day 4 @ 30% Max Speed 1: _____	3m
4-3-1	Day 1 @ 80% Max Speed 2: _____	3m
2-4-3	Day 2 @ 80% Max Speed 2: _____	3m
1-2-4	Day 3 @ 80% Max Speed 2: _____	3m
4-1-2	Day 4 @ 80% Max Speed 2: _____	3m
3-4-1	Day 5 @ 80% Max Speed 2: _____	3m
2-3-4	Day 3 @ 90% Max Speed 3: _____	3m

DAY 45	Date __ / __ / ____	
EXERCISE PERMUTATION ASCENDING/DESCENDING	EXERCISE DETAIL and METRONOME SPEED SETTING	TIME
3-1-2	Day 5 @ 30% Max Speed 1: _____	3m
4-3-1	Day 2 @ 80% Max Speed 2: _____	3m
2-4-3	Day 3 @ 80% Max Speed 2: _____	3m
1-2-4	Day 4 @ 80% Max Speed 2: _____	3m
4-1-2	Day 5 @ 80% Max Speed 2: _____	3m
3-4-1	Max Speed 3: _____	
2-3-4	Day 4 @ 90% Max Speed 3: _____	3m

DAY 46	Date __ / __ / ____	
EXERCISE PERMUTATION ASCENDING/DESCENDING	EXERCISE DETAIL and METRONOME SPEED SETTING	TIME
3-1-2	Day 1 @ 50% Max Speed 1: _____	3m
4-3-1	Day 3 @ 80% Max Speed 2: _____	3m
2-4-3	Day 4 @ 80% Max Speed 2: _____	3m
1-2-4	Day 5 @ 80% Max Speed 2: _____	3m
4-1-2	Max Speed 3: _____	
3-4-1	Day 1 @ 90% Max Speed 3: _____	3m
2-3-4	Day 5 @ 90% Max Speed 3: _____	3m

DAY 47		Date __ / __ / ____
EXERCISE PERMUTATION ASCENDING/DESCENDING	EXERCISE DETAIL and METRONOME SPEED SETTING	TIME
3-1-2	Day 2 @ 50% Max Speed 1: _____	3m
4-3-1	Day 4 @ 80% Max Speed 2: _____	3m
2-4-3	Day 5 @ 80% Max Speed 2: _____	3m
1-2-4	Max Speed 3: _____	
4-1-2	Day 1 @ 90% Max Speed 3: _____	3m
3-4-1	Day 2 @ 90% Max Speed 3: _____	3m
2-3-4	Max Speed 4: _____ Maintenance Level	

DAY 48		Date __ / __ / ____
EXERCISE PERMUTATION ASCENDING/DESCENDING	EXERCISE DETAIL and METRONOME SPEED SETTING	TIME
1-3-2	Max Speed 1: _____	
3-1-2	Day 3 @ 50% Max Speed 1: _____	3m
4-3-1	Day 5 @ 80% Max Speed 2: _____	3m
2-4-3	Max Speed 3: _____	
1-2-4	Day 1 @ 90% Max Speed 3: _____	3m
4-1-2	Day 2 @ 90% Max Speed 3: _____	3m
3-4-1	Day 3 @ 90% Max Speed 3: _____	3m

DAY 49		Date __ / __ / ____
EXERCISE PERMUTATION ASCENDING/DESCENDING	EXERCISE DETAIL and METRONOME SPEED SETTING	TIME
1-3-2	Day 1 @ 30% Max Speed 1: _____	3m
3-1-2	Day 1 @ 65% Max Speed 1: _____	3m
4-3-1	Max Speed 3: _____	
2-4-3	Day 1 @ 90% Max Speed 3: _____	3m
1-2-4	Day 2 @ 90% Max Speed 3: _____	3m
4-1-2	Day 3 @ 90% Max Speed 3: _____	3m
3-4-1	Day 4 @ 90% Max Speed 3: _____	3m

DAY 50	Date __ /__ /____	
EXERCISE PERMUTATION ASCENDING/DESCENDING	EXERCISE DETAIL and METRONOME SPEED SETTING	TIME
1-3-2	Day 2 @ 30% Max Speed 1: _____	3m
3-1-2	Day 2 @ 65% Max Speed 1: _____	3m
4-3-1	Day 1 @ 90% Max Speed 3: _____	3m
2-4-3	Day 2 @ 90% Max Speed 3: _____	3m
1-2-4	Day 3 @ 90% Max Speed 3: _____	3m
4-1-2	Day 4 @ 90% Max Speed 3: _____	3m
3-4-1	Day 5 @ 90% Max Speed 3: _____	3m

DAY 51	Date __ /__ /____	
EXERCISE PERMUTATION ASCENDING/DESCENDING	EXERCISE DETAIL and METRONOME SPEED SETTING	TIME
1-3-2	Day 3 @ 30% Max Speed 1: _____	3m
3-1-2	Day 3 @ 65% Max Speed 1: _____	3m
4-3-1	Day 2 @ 90% Max Speed 3: _____	3m
2-4-3	Day 3 @ 90% Max Speed 3: _____	3m
1-2-4	Day 4 @ 90% Max Speed 3: _____	3m
4-1-2	Day 5 @ 90% Max Speed 3: _____	3m
3-4-1	Max Speed 4: _____ Maintenance Level	

DAY 52	Date __ /__ /____	
EXERCISE PERMUTATION ASCENDING/DESCENDING	EXERCISE DETAIL and METRONOME SPEED SETTING	TIME
3-2-4	Max Speed 1: _____	
1-3-2	Day 4 @ 30% Max Speed 1: _____	3m
3-1-2	Max Speed 2: _____	
4-3-1	Day 3 @ 90% Max Speed 3: _____	3m
2-4-3	Day 4 @ 90% Max Speed 3: _____	3m
1-2-4	Day 5 @ 90% Max Speed 3: _____	3m
4-1-2	Max Speed 4: _____ Maintenance Level	

DAY 53		Date __ /__ /____
EXERCISE PERMUTATION ASCENDING/DESCENDING	EXERCISE DETAIL and METRONOME SPEED SETTING	TIME
2-4-1	Max Speed 1: _____	
3-2-4	Day 1 @ 30% Max Speed 1: _____	3m
1-3-2	Day 5 @ 30% Max Speed 1: _____	3m
3-1-2	Day 1 @ 80% Max Speed 2: _____	3m
4-3-1	Day 4 @ 90% Max Speed 3: _____	3m
2-4-3	Day 5 @ 90% Max Speed 3: _____	3m
1-2-4	Max Speed 4: _____ Maintenance Level	

DAY 54		Date __ /__ /____
EXERCISE PERMUTATION ASCENDING/DESCENDING	EXERCISE DETAIL and METRONOME SPEED SETTING	TIME
4-1-3	Max Speed 1: _____	
2-4-1	Day 1 @ 30% Max Speed 1: _____	3m
3-2-4	Day 2 @ 30% Max Speed 1: _____	3m
1-3-2	Day 1 @ 50% Max Speed 1: _____	3m
3-1-2	Day 2 @ 80% Max Speed 2: _____	3m
4-3-1	Day 5 @ 90% Max Speed 3: _____	3m
2-4-3	Max Speed 4: _____ Maintenance Level	

DAY 55		Date __ /__ /____
EXERCISE PERMUTATION ASCENDING/DESCENDING	EXERCISE DETAIL and METRONOME SPEED SETTING	TIME
1-3-4	Max Speed 1: _____	
4-1-3	Day 1 @ 30% Max Speed 1: _____	3m
2-4-1	Day 2 @ 30% Max Speed 1: _____	3m
3-2-4	Day 3 @ 30% Max Speed 1: _____	3m
1-3-2	Day 2 @ 50% Max Speed 1: _____	3m
3-1-2	Day 3 @ 80% Max Speed 2: _____	3m
4-3-1	Max Speed 4: _____ Maintenance Level	

DAY 56	Date __ / __ / ____	
EXERCISE PERMUTATION ASCENDING/DESCENDING	EXERCISE DETAIL and METRONOME SPEED SETTING	TIME
3-4-2	Max Speed 1: _____	
1-3-4	Day 1 @ 30% Max Speed 1: _____	3m
4-1-3	Day 2 @ 30% Max Speed 1: _____	3m
2-4-1	Day 3 @ 30% Max Speed 1: _____	3m
3-2-4	Day 4 @ 30% Max Speed 1: _____	3m
1-3-2	Day 3 @ 50% Max Speed 1: _____	3m
3-1-2	Day 4 @ 80% Max Speed 2: _____	3m

DAY 57	Date __ / __ / ____	
EXERCISE PERMUTATION ASCENDING/DESCENDING	EXERCISE DETAIL and METRONOME SPEED SETTING	TIME
3-4-2	Day 1 @ 30% Max Speed 1: _____	3m
1-3-4	Day 2 @ 30% Max Speed 1: _____	3m
4-1-3	Day 3 @ 30% Max Speed 1: _____	3m
2-4-1	Day 4 @ 30% Max Speed 1: _____	3m
3-2-4	Day 5 @ 30% Max Speed 1: _____	3m
1-3-2	Day 1 @ 65% Max Speed 1: _____	3m
3-1-2	Day 5 @ 80% Max Speed 2: _____	3m

DAY 58	Date __ / __ / ____	
EXERCISE PERMUTATION ASCENDING/DESCENDING	EXERCISE DETAIL and METRONOME SPEED SETTING	TIME
3-4-2	Day 2 @ 30% Max Speed 1: _____	3m
1-3-4	Day 3 @ 30% Max Speed 1: _____	3m
4-1-3	Day 4 @ 30% Max Speed 1: _____	3m
2-4-1	Day 5 @ 30% Max Speed 1: _____	3m
3-2-4	Day 1 @ 50% Max Speed 1: _____	3m
1-3-2	Day 2 @ 65% Max Speed 1: _____	3m
3-1-2	Max Speed 3: _____	

DAY 59	Date __ / __ / ____	
EXERCISE PERMUTATION ASCENDING/DESCENDING	EXERCISE DETAIL and METRONOME SPEED SETTING	TIME
3-4-2	Day 3 @ 30% Max Speed 1: _____	3m
1-3-4	Day 4 @ 30% Max Speed 1: _____	3m
4-1-3	Day 5 @ 30% Max Speed 1: _____	3m
2-4-1	Day 1 @ 50% Max Speed 1: _____	3m
3-2-4	Day 2 @ 50% Max Speed 1: _____	3m
1-3-2	Day 3 @ 65% Max Speed 1: _____	3m
3-1-2	Day 1 @ 90% Max Speed 3: _____	3m

DAY 60	Date __ / __ / ____	
EXERCISE PERMUTATION ASCENDING/DESCENDING	EXERCISE DETAIL and METRONOME SPEED SETTING	TIME
3-4-2	Day 4 @ 30% Max Speed 1: _____	3m
1-3-4	Day 5 @ 30% Max Speed 1: _____	3m
4-1-3	Day 1 @ 50% Max Speed 1: _____	3m
2-4-1	Day 2 @ 50% Max Speed 1: _____	3m
3-2-4	Day 3 @ 50% Max Speed 1: _____	3m
1-3-2	Max Speed 2: _____	
3-1-2	Day 2 @ 90% Max Speed 3: _____	3m

DAY 61	Date __ / __ / ____	
EXERCISE PERMUTATION ASCENDING/DESCENDING	EXERCISE DETAIL and METRONOME SPEED SETTING	TIME
3-4-2	Day 5 @ 30% Max Speed 1: _____	3m
1-3-4	Day 1 @ 50% Max Speed 1: _____	3m
4-1-3	Day 2 @ 50% Max Speed 1: _____	3m
2-4-1	Day 3 @ 50% Max Speed 1: _____	3m
3-2-4	Day 1 @ 65% Max Speed 1: _____	3m
1-3-2	Day 1 @ 80% Max Speed 2: _____	3m
3-1-2	Day 3 @ 90% Max Speed 3: _____	3m

DAY 62	Date __ / __ / ____	
EXERCISE PERMUTATION ASCENDING/DESCENDING	EXERCISE DETAIL and METRONOME SPEED SETTING	TIME
3-4-2	Day 1 @ 50% Max Speed 1: _____	3m
1-3-4	Day 2 @ 50% Max Speed 1: _____	3m
4-1-3	Day 3 @ 50% Max Speed 1: _____	3m
2-4-1	Day 1 @ 65% Max Speed 1: _____	3m
3-2-4	Day 2 @ 65% Max Speed 1: _____	3m
1-3-2	Day 2 @ 80% Max Speed 2: _____	3m
3-1-2	Day 4 @ 90% Max Speed 3: _____	3m

DAY 63	Date __ / __ / ____	
EXERCISE PERMUTATION ASCENDING/DESCENDING	EXERCISE DETAIL and METRONOME SPEED SETTING	TIME
3-4-2	Day 2 @ 50% Max Speed 1: _____	3m
1-3-4	Day 3 @ 50% Max Speed 1: _____	3m
4-1-3	Day 1 @ 65% Max Speed 1: _____	3m
2-4-1	Day 2 @ 65% Max Speed 1: _____	3m
3-2-4	Day 3 @ 65% Max Speed 1: _____	3m
1-3-2	Day 3 @ 80% Max Speed 2: _____	3m
3-1-2	Day 5 @ 90% Max Speed 3: _____	3m

DAY 64	Date __ / __ / ____	
EXERCISE PERMUTATION ASCENDING/DESCENDING	EXERCISE DETAIL and METRONOME SPEED SETTING	TIME
3-4-2	Day 3 @ 50% Max Speed 1: _____	3m
1-3-4	Day 1 @ 65% Max Speed 1: _____	3m
4-1-3	Day 2 @ 65% Max Speed 1: _____	3m
2-4-1	Day 3 @ 65% Max Speed 1: _____	3m
3-2-4	Max Speed 2: _____	
1-3-2	Day 4 @ 80% Max Speed 2: _____	3m
3-1-2	Max Speed 4: _____ Maintenance Level	

DAY 65	Date __ / __ / ____	
EXERCISE PERMUTATION ASCENDING/DESCENDING	EXERCISE DETAIL and METRONOME SPEED SETTING	TIME
4-2-1	Max Speed 1: _____	
3-4-2	Day 1 @ 65% Max Speed 1: _____	3m
1-3-4	Day 2 @ 65% Max Speed 1: _____	3m
4-1-3	Day 3 @ 65% Max Speed 1: _____	3m
2-4-1	Max Speed 2: _____	
3-2-4	Day 1 @ 80% Max Speed 2: _____	3m
1-3-2	Day 5 @ 80% Max Speed 2: _____	3m

DAY 66	Date __ / __ / ____	
EXERCISE PERMUTATION ASCENDING/DESCENDING	EXERCISE DETAIL and METRONOME SPEED SETTING	TIME
4-2-1	Day 1 @ 30% Max Speed 1: _____	3m
3-4-2	Day 2 @ 65% Max Speed 1: _____	3m
1-3-4	Day 3 @ 65% Max Speed 1: _____	3m
4-1-3	Max Speed 2: _____	
2-4-1	Day 1 @ 80% Max Speed 2: _____	3m
3-2-4	Day 2 @ 80% Max Speed 2: _____	3m
1-3-2	Max Speed 3: _____	

DAY 67	Date __ / __ / ____	
EXERCISE PERMUTATION ASCENDING/DESCENDING	EXERCISE DETAIL and METRONOME SPEED SETTING	TIME
4-2-1	Day 2 @ 30% Max Speed 1: _____	3m
3-4-2	Day 3 @ 65% Max Speed 1: _____	3m
1-3-4	Max Speed 2: _____	
4-1-3	Day 1 @ 80% Max Speed 2: _____	3m
2-4-1	Day 2 @ 80% Max Speed 2: _____	3m
3-2-4	Day 3 @ 80% Max Speed 2: _____	3m
1-3-2	Day 1 @ 90% Max Speed 3: _____	3m

DAY 68	Date __ / __ / ____	
EXERCISE PERMUTATION ASCENDING/DESCENDING	EXERCISE DETAIL and METRONOME SPEED SETTING	TIME
4-2-1	Day 3 @ 30% Max Speed 1: _____	3m
3-4-2	Max Speed 2: _____	
1-3-4	Day 1 @ 80% Max Speed 2: _____	3m
4-1-3	Day 2 @ 80% Max Speed 2: _____	3m
2-4-1	Day 3 @ 80% Max Speed 2: _____	3m
3-2-4	Day 4 @ 80% Max Speed 2: _____	3m
1-3-2	Day 2 @ 90% Max Speed 3: _____	3m

DAY 69	Date __ / __ / ____	
EXERCISE PERMUTATION ASCENDING/DESCENDING	EXERCISE DETAIL and METRONOME SPEED SETTING	TIME
4-2-1	Day 4 @ 30% Max Speed 1: _____	3m
3-4-2	Day 1 @ 80% Max Speed 2: _____	3m
1-3-4	Day 2 @ 80% Max Speed 2: _____	3m
4-1-3	Day 3 @ 80% Max Speed 2: _____	3m
2-4-1	Day 4 @ 80% Max Speed 2: _____	3m
3-2-4	Day 5 @ 80% Max Speed 2: _____	3m
1-3-2	Day 3 @ 90% Max Speed 3: _____	3m

DAY 70	Date __ / __ / ____	
EXERCISE PERMUTATION ASCENDING/DESCENDING	EXERCISE DETAIL and METRONOME SPEED SETTING	TIME
4-2-1	Day 5 @ 30% Max Speed 1: _____	3m
3-4-2	Day 2 @ 80% Max Speed 2: _____	3m
1-3-4	Day 3 @ 80% Max Speed 2: _____	3m
4-1-3	Day 4 @ 80% Max Speed 2: _____	3m
2-4-1	Day 5 @ 80% Max Speed 2: _____	3m
3-2-4	Max Speed 3: _____	
1-3-2	Day 4 @ 90% Max Speed 3: _____	3m

DAY 71	Date __ / __ / ____	
EXERCISE PERMUTATION ASCENDING/DESCENDING	EXERCISE DETAIL and METRONOME SPEED SETTING	TIME
4-2-1	Day 1 @ 50% Max Speed 1: _____	3m
3-4-2	Day 3 @ 80% Max Speed 2: _____	3m
1-3-4	Day 4 @ 80% Max Speed 2: _____	3m
4-1-3	Day 5 @ 80% Max Speed 2: _____	3m
2-4-1	Max Speed 3: _____	
3-2-4	Day 1 @ 90% Max Speed 3: _____	3m
1-3-2	Day 5 @ 90% Max Speed 3: _____	3m

DAY 72	Date __ / __ / ____	
EXERCISE PERMUTATION ASCENDING/DESCENDING	EXERCISE DETAIL and METRONOME SPEED SETTING	TIME
4-2-1	Day 2 @ 50% Max Speed 1: _____	3m
3-4-2	Day 4 @ 80% Max Speed 2: _____	3m
1-3-4	Day 5 @ 80% Max Speed 2: _____	3m
4-1-3	Max Speed 3: _____	
2-4-1	Day 1 @ 90% Max Speed 3: _____	3m
3-2-4	Day 2 @ 90% Max Speed 3: _____	3m
1-3-2	Max Speed 4: _____ Maintenance Level	

DAY 73	Date __ / __ / ____	
EXERCISE PERMUTATION ASCENDING/DESCENDING	EXERCISE DETAIL and METRONOME SPEED SETTING	TIME
2-1-3	Max Speed 1: _____	
4-2-1	Day 3 @ 50% Max Speed 1: _____	3m
3-4-2	Day 5 @ 80% Max Speed 2: _____	3m
1-3-4	Max Speed 3: _____	
4-1-3	Day 1 @ 90% Max Speed 3: _____	3m
2-4-1	Day 2 @ 90% Max Speed 3: _____	3m
3-2-4	Day 3 @ 90% Max Speed 3: _____	3m

DAY 74	Date __ / __ / ____	
EXERCISE PERMUTATION ASCENDING/DESCENDING	EXERCISE DETAIL and METRONOME SPEED SETTING	TIME
2-1-3	Day 1 @ 30% Max Speed 1: _____	3m
4-2-1	Day 1 @ 65% Max Speed 1: _____	3m
3-4-2	Max Speed 3: _____	
1-3-4	Day 1 @ 90% Max Speed 3: _____	3m
4-1-3	Day 2 @ 90% Max Speed 3: _____	3m
2-4-1	Day 3 @ 90% Max Speed 3: _____	3m
3-2-4	Day 4 @ 90% Max Speed 3: _____	3m

DAY 75	Date __ / __ / ____	
EXERCISE PERMUTATION ASCENDING/DESCENDING	EXERCISE DETAIL and METRONOME SPEED SETTING	TIME
2-1-3	Day 2 @ 30% Max Speed 1: _____	3m
4-2-1	Day 2 @ 65% Max Speed 1: _____	3m
3-4-2	Day 1 @ 90% Max Speed 3: _____	3m
1-3-4	Day 2 @ 90% Max Speed 3: _____	3m
4-1-3	Day 3 @ 90% Max Speed 3: _____	3m
2-4-1	Day 4 @ 90% Max Speed 3: _____	3m
3-2-4	Day 5 @ 90% Max Speed 3: _____	3m

DAY 76	Date __ / __ / ____	
EXERCISE PERMUTATION ASCENDING/DESCENDING	EXERCISE DETAIL and METRONOME SPEED SETTING	TIME
2-1-3	Day 3 @ 30% Max Speed 1: _____	3m
4-2-1	Day 3 @ 65% Max Speed 1: _____	3m
3-4-2	Day 2 @ 90% Max Speed 3: _____	3m
1-3-4	Day 3 @ 90% Max Speed 3: _____	3m
4-1-3	Day 4 @ 90% Max Speed 3: _____	3m
2-4-1	Day 5 @ 90% Max Speed 3: _____	3m
3-2-4	Max Speed 4: _____ Maintenance Level	

DAY 77		Date __ /__ /____
EXERCISE PERMUTATION ASCENDING/DESCENDING	EXERCISE DETAIL and METRONOME SPEED SETTING	TIME
1-4-2	Max Speed 1: _____	
2-1-3	Day 4 @ 30% Max Speed 1: _____	3m
4-2-1	Max Speed 2: _____	
3-4-2	Day 3 @ 90% Max Speed 3: _____	3m
1-3-4	Day 4 @ 90% Max Speed 3: _____	3m
4-1-3	Day 5 @ 90% Max Speed 3: _____	3m
2-4-1	Max Speed 4: _____ Maintenance Level	

DAY 78		Date __ /__ /____
EXERCISE PERMUTATION ASCENDING/DESCENDING	EXERCISE DETAIL and METRONOME SPEED SETTING	TIME
4-2-3	Max Speed 1: _____	
1-4-2	Day 1 @ 30% Max Speed 1: _____	3m
2-1-3	Day 5 @ 30% Max Speed 1: _____	3m
4-2-1	Day 1 @ 80% Max Speed 2: _____	3m
3-4-2	Day 4 @ 90% Max Speed 3: _____	3m
1-3-4	Day 5 @ 90% Max Speed 3: _____	3m
4-1-3	Max Speed 4: _____ Maintenance Level	

DAY 79		Date __ /__ /____
EXERCISE PERMUTATION ASCENDING/DESCENDING	EXERCISE DETAIL and METRONOME SPEED SETTING	TIME
2-3-1	Max Speed 1: _____	
4-2-3	Day 1 @ 30% Max Speed 1: _____	3m
1-4-2	Day 2 @ 30% Max Speed 1: _____	3m
2-1-3	Day 1 @ 50% Max Speed 1: _____	3m
4-2-1	Day 2 @ 80% Max Speed 2: _____	3m
3-4-2	Day 5 @ 90% Max Speed 3: _____	3m
1-3-4	Max Speed 4: _____ Maintenance Level	

DAY 80	Date __ / __ / ____	
EXERCISE PERMUTATION ASCENDING/DESCENDING	EXERCISE DETAIL and METRONOME SPEED SETTING	TIME
3-1-4	Max Speed 1: _____	
2-3-1	Day 1 @ 30% Max Speed 1: _____	3m
4-2-3	Day 2 @ 30% Max Speed 1: _____	3m
1-4-2	Day 3 @ 30% Max Speed 1: _____	3m
2-1-3	Day 2 @ 50% Max Speed 1: _____	3m
4-2-1	Day 3 @ 80% Max Speed 2: _____	3m
3-4-2	Max Speed 4: _____ Maintenance Level	

DAY 81	Date __ / __ / ____	
EXERCISE PERMUTATION ASCENDING/DESCENDING	EXERCISE DETAIL and METRONOME SPEED SETTING	TIME
1-4-3	Max Speed 1: _____	
3-1-4	Day 1 @ 30% Max Speed 1: _____	3m
2-3-1	Day 2 @ 30% Max Speed 1: _____	3m
4-2-3	Day 3 @ 30% Max Speed 1: _____	3m
1-4-2	Day 4 @ 30% Max Speed 1: _____	3m
2-1-3	Day 3 @ 50% Max Speed 1: _____	3m
4-2-1	Day 4 @ 80% Max Speed 2: _____	3m

DAY 82	Date __ / __ / ____	
EXERCISE PERMUTATION ASCENDING/DESCENDING	EXERCISE DETAIL and METRONOME SPEED SETTING	TIME
1-4-3	Day 1 @ 30% Max Speed 1: _____	3m
3-1-4	Day 2 @ 30% Max Speed 1: _____	3m
2-3-1	Day 3 @ 30% Max Speed 1: _____	3m
4-2-3	Day 4 @ 30% Max Speed 1: _____	3m
1-4-2	Day 5 @ 30% Max Speed 1: _____	3m
2-1-3	Day 1 @ 65% Max Speed 1: _____	3m
4-2-1	Day 5 @ 80% Max Speed 2: _____	3m

DAY 83	Date __ /__ /____	
EXERCISE PERMUTATION ASCENDING/DESCENDING	EXERCISE DETAIL and METRONOME SPEED SETTING	TIME
1-4-3	Day 2 @ 30% Max Speed 1: _____	3m
3-1-4	Day 3 @ 30% Max Speed 1: _____	3m
2-3-1	Day 4 @ 30% Max Speed 1: _____	3m
4-2-3	Day 5 @ 30% Max Speed 1: _____	3m
1-4-2	Day 1 @ 50% Max Speed 1: _____	3m
2-1-3	Day 2 @ 65% Max Speed 1: _____	3m
4-2-1	Max Speed 3: _____	

DAY 84	Date __ /__ /____	
EXERCISE PERMUTATION ASCENDING/DESCENDING	EXERCISE DETAIL and METRONOME SPEED SETTING	TIME
1-4-3	Day 3 @ 30% Max Speed 1: _____	3m
3-1-4	Day 4 @ 30% Max Speed 1: _____	3m
2-3-1	Day 5 @ 30% Max Speed 1: _____	3m
4-2-3	Day 1 @ 50% Max Speed 1: _____	3m
1-4-2	Day 2 @ 50% Max Speed 1: _____	3m
2-1-3	Day 3 @ 65% Max Speed 1: _____	3m
4-2-1	Day 1 @ 90% Max Speed 3: _____	3m

DAY 85	Date __ /__ /____	
EXERCISE PERMUTATION ASCENDING/DESCENDING	EXERCISE DETAIL and METRONOME SPEED SETTING	TIME
1-4-3	Day 4 @ 30% Max Speed 1: _____	3m
3-1-4	Day 5 @ 30% Max Speed 1: _____	3m
2-3-1	Day 1 @ 50% Max Speed 1: _____	3m
4-2-3	Day 2 @ 50% Max Speed 1: _____	3m
1-4-2	Day 3 @ 50% Max Speed 1: _____	3m
2-1-3	Max Speed 2: _____	
4-2-1	Day 2 @ 90% Max Speed 3: _____	3m

DAY 86	Date __ / __ / ____	
EXERCISE PERMUTATION ASCENDING/DESCENDING	EXERCISE DETAIL and METRONOME SPEED SETTING	TIME
1-4-3	Day 5 @ 30% Max Speed 1: _____	3m
3-1-4	Day 1 @ 50% Max Speed 1: _____	3m
2-3-1	Day 2 @ 50% Max Speed 1: _____	3m
4-2-3	Day 3 @ 50% Max Speed 1: _____	3m
1-4-2	Day 1 @ 65% Max Speed 1: _____	3m
2-1-3	Day 1 @ 80% Max Speed 2: _____	3m
4-2-1	Day 3 @ 90% Max Speed 3: _____	3m

DAY 87	Date __ / __ / ____	
EXERCISE PERMUTATION ASCENDING/DESCENDING	EXERCISE DETAIL and METRONOME SPEED SETTING	TIME
1-4-3	Day 1 @ 50% Max Speed 1: _____	3m
3-1-4	Day 2 @ 50% Max Speed 1: _____	3m
2-3-1	Day 3 @ 50% Max Speed 1: _____	3m
4-2-3	Day 1 @ 65% Max Speed 1: _____	3m
1-4-2	Day 2 @ 65% Max Speed 1: _____	3m
2-1-3	Day 2 @ 80% Max Speed 2: _____	3m
4-2-1	Day 4 @ 90% Max Speed 3: _____	3m

DAY 88	Date __ / __ / ____	
EXERCISE PERMUTATION ASCENDING/DESCENDING	EXERCISE DETAIL and METRONOME SPEED SETTING	TIME
1-4-3	Day 2 @ 50% Max Speed 1: _____	3m
3-1-4	Day 3 @ 50% Max Speed 1: _____	3m
2-3-1	Day 1 @ 65% Max Speed 1: _____	3m
4-2-3	Day 2 @ 65% Max Speed 1: _____	3m
1-4-2	Day 3 @ 65% Max Speed 1: _____	3m
2-1-3	Day 3 @ 80% Max Speed 2: _____	3m
4-2-1	Day 5 @ 90% Max Speed 3: _____	3m

DAY 89	Date __ / __ / ____	
EXERCISE PERMUTATION ASCENDING/DESCENDING	EXERCISE DETAIL and METRONOME SPEED SETTING	TIME
1-4-3	Day 3 @ 50% Max Speed 1: _____	3m
3-1-4	Day 1 @ 65% Max Speed 1: _____	3m
2-3-1	Day 2 @ 65% Max Speed 1: _____	3m
4-2-3	Day 3 @ 65% Max Speed 1: _____	3m
1-4-2	Max Speed 2: _____	
2-1-3	Day 4 @ 80% Max Speed 2: _____	3m
4-2-1	Max Speed 4: _____ Maintenance Level	

DAY 90	Date __ / __ / ____	
EXERCISE PERMUTATION ASCENDING/DESCENDING	EXERCISE DETAIL and METRONOME SPEED SETTING	TIME
4-3-2	Max Speed 1: _____	
1-4-3	Day 3 @ 50% Max Speed 1: _____	3m
3-1-4	Day 1 @ 65% Max Speed 1: _____	3m
2-3-1	Day 2 @ 65% Max Speed 1: _____	3m
4-2-3	Day 3 @ 65% Max Speed 1: _____	3m
1-4-2	Max Speed 2: _____	
2-1-3	Day 4 @ 80% Max Speed 2: _____	3m

DAY 91	Date __ / __ / ____	
EXERCISE PERMUTATION ASCENDING/DESCENDING	EXERCISE DETAIL and METRONOME SPEED SETTING	TIME
4-3-2	Day 1 @ 30% Max Speed 1: _____	3m
1-4-3	Day 1 @ 65% Max Speed 1: _____	3m
3-1-4	Day 2 @ 65% Max Speed 1: _____	3m
2-3-1	Day 3 @ 65% Max Speed 1: _____	3m
4-2-3	Max Speed 2: _____	
1-4-2	Day 1 @ 80% Max Speed 2: _____	3m
2-1-3	Day 5 @ 80% Max Speed 2: _____	3m

DAY 92	Date __ / __ / ____	
EXERCISE PERMUTATION ASCENDING/DESCENDING	EXERCISE DETAIL and METRONOME SPEED SETTING	TIME
4-3-2	Day 2 @ 30% Max Speed 1: _____	3m
1-4-3	Day 2 @ 65% Max Speed 1: _____	3m
3-1-4	Day 3 @ 65% Max Speed 1: _____	3m
2-3-1	Max Speed 2: _____	
4-2-3	Day 1 @ 80% Max Speed 2: _____	3m
1-4-2	Day 2 @ 80% Max Speed 2: _____	3m
2-1-3	Max Speed 3: _____	

DAY 93	Date __ / __ / ____	
EXERCISE PERMUTATION ASCENDING/DESCENDING	EXERCISE DETAIL and METRONOME SPEED SETTING	TIME
4-3-2	Day 3 @ 30% Max Speed 1: _____	3m
1-4-3	Day 3 @ 65% Max Speed 1: _____	3m
3-1-4	Max Speed 2: _____	
2-3-1	Day 1 @ 80% Max Speed 2: _____	3m
4-2-3	Day 2 @ 80% Max Speed 2: _____	3m
1-4-2	Day 3 @ 80% Max Speed 2: _____	3m
2-1-3	Day 1 @ 90% Max Speed 3: _____	3m

DAY 94	Date __ / __ / ____	
EXERCISE PERMUTATION ASCENDING/DESCENDING	EXERCISE DETAIL and METRONOME SPEED SETTING	TIME
4-3-2	Day 4 @ 30% Max Speed 1: _____	3m
1-4-3	Max Speed 2: _____	
3-1-4	Day 1 @ 80% Max Speed 2: _____	3m
2-3-1	Day 2 @ 80% Max Speed 2: _____	3m
4-2-3	Day 3 @ 80% Max Speed 2: _____	3m
1-4-2	Day 4 @ 80% Max Speed 2: _____	3m
2-1-3	Day 2 @ 90% Max Speed 3: _____	3m

DAY 95	Date __ / __ / ____	
EXERCISE PERMUTATION ASCENDING/DESCENDING	EXERCISE DETAIL and METRONOME SPEED SETTING	TIME
4-3-2	Day 5 @ 30% Max Speed 1: _____	3m
1-4-3	Day 1 @ 80% Max Speed 2: _____	3m
3-1-4	Day 2 @ 80% Max Speed 2: _____	3m
2-3-1	Day 3 @ 80% Max Speed 2: _____	3m
4-2-3	Day 4 @ 80% Max Speed 2: _____	3m
1-4-2	Day 5 @ 80% Max Speed 2: _____	3m
2-1-3	Day 3 @ 90% Max Speed 3: _____	3m

DAY 96	Date __ / __ / ____	
EXERCISE PERMUTATION ASCENDING/DESCENDING	EXERCISE DETAIL and METRONOME SPEED SETTING	TIME
4-3-2	Day 1 @ 50% Max Speed 1: _____	3m
1-4-3	Day 2 @ 80% Max Speed 2: _____	3m
3-1-4	Day 3 @ 80% Max Speed 2: _____	3m
2-3-1	Day 4 @ 80% Max Speed 2: _____	3m
4-2-3	Day 5 @ 80% Max Speed 2: _____	3m
1-4-2	Max Speed 3: _____	
2-1-3	Day 4 @ 90% Max Speed 3: _____	3m

DAY 97	Date __ / __ / ____	
EXERCISE PERMUTATION ASCENDING/DESCENDING	EXERCISE DETAIL and METRONOME SPEED SETTING	TIME
4-3-2	Day 2 @ 50% Max Speed 1: _____	3m
1-4-3	Day 3 @ 80% Max Speed 2: _____	3m
3-1-4	Day 4 @ 80% Max Speed 2: _____	3m
2-3-1	Day 5 @ 80% Max Speed 2: _____	3m
4-2-3	Max Speed 3: _____	
1-4-2	Day 1 @ 90% Max Speed 3: _____	3m
2-1-3	Day 5 @ 90% Max Speed 3: _____	3m

DAY 98	Date __ / __ / ____	
EXERCISE PERMUTATION ASCENDING/DESCENDING	EXERCISE DETAIL and METRONOME SPEED SETTING	TIME
4-3-2	Day 3 @ 50% Max Speed 1: _____	3m
1-4-3	Day 4 @ 80% Max Speed 2: _____	3m
3-1-4	Day 5 @ 80% Max Speed 2: _____	3m
2-3-1	Max Speed 3: _____	
4-2-3	Day 1 @ 90% Max Speed 3: _____	3m
1-4-2	Day 2 @ 90% Max Speed 3: _____	3m
2-1-3	Max Speed 4: _____ Maintenance Level	

DAY 99	Date __ / __ / ____	
EXERCISE PERMUTATION ASCENDING/DESCENDING	EXERCISE DETAIL and METRONOME SPEED SETTING	TIME
3-2-1	Max Speed 1: _____	
4-3-2	Day 1 @ 65% Max Speed 1: _____	3m
1-4-3	Day 5 @ 80% Max Speed 2: _____	3m
3-1-4	Max Speed 3: _____	
2-3-1	Day 1 @ 90% Max Speed 3: _____	3m
4-2-3	Day 2 @ 90% Max Speed 3: _____	3m
1-4-2	Day 3 @ 90% Max Speed 3: _____	3m

DAY 100	Date __ / __ / ____	
EXERCISE PERMUTATION ASCENDING/DESCENDING	EXERCISE DETAIL and METRONOME SPEED SETTING	TIME
3-2-1	Day 1 @ 30% Max Speed 1: _____	3m
4-3-2	Day 2 @ 65% Max Speed 1: _____	3m
1-4-3	Max Speed 3: _____	
3-1-4	Day 1 @ 90% Max Speed 3: _____	3m
2-3-1	Day 2 @ 90% Max Speed 3: _____	3m
4-2-3	Day 3 @ 90% Max Speed 3: _____	3m
1-4-2	Day 4 @ 90% Max Speed 3: _____	3m

DAY 101		Date __ / __ / ____
EXERCISE PERMUTATION ASCENDING/DESCENDING	EXERCISE DETAIL and METRONOME SPEED SETTING	TIME
3-2-1	Day 2 @ 30% Max Speed 1: _____	3m
4-3-2	Day 3 @ 65% Max Speed 1: _____	3m
1-4-3	Day 1 @ 90% Max Speed 3: _____	3m
3-1-4	Day 2 @ 90% Max Speed 3: _____	3m
2-3-1	Day 3 @ 90% Max Speed 3: _____	3m
4-2-3	Day 4 @ 90% Max Speed 3: _____	3m
1-4-2	Day 5 @ 90% Max Speed 3: _____	3m

DAY 101		Date __ / __ / ____
EXERCISE PERMUTATION ASCENDING/DESCENDING	EXERCISE DETAIL and METRONOME SPEED SETTING	TIME
3-2-1	Day 3 @ 30% Max Speed 1: _____	3m
4-3-2	Max Speed 2: _____	
1-4-3	Day 2 @ 90% Max Speed 3: _____	3m
3-1-4	Day 3 @ 90% Max Speed 3: _____	3m
2-3-1	Day 4 @ 90% Max Speed 3: _____	3m
4-2-3	Day 5 @ 90% Max Speed 3: _____	3m
1-4-2	Max Speed 4: _____ Maintenance Level	

DAY 102		Date __ / __ / ____
EXERCISE PERMUTATION ASCENDING/DESCENDING	EXERCISE DETAIL and METRONOME SPEED SETTING	TIME
2-1-4	Max Speed 1: _____	
3-2-1	Day 4 @ 30% Max Speed 1: _____	3m
4-3-2	Day 1 @ 80% Max Speed 2: _____	3m
1-4-3	Day 3 @ 90% Max Speed 3: _____	3m
3-1-4	Day 4 @ 90% Max Speed 3: _____	3m
2-3-1	Day 5 @ 90% Max Speed 3: _____	3m
4-2-3	Max Speed 4: _____ Maintenance Level	

DAY 103	Date __ / __ / ____	
EXERCISE PERMUTATION ASCENDING/DESCENDING	EXERCISE DETAIL and METRONOME SPEED SETTING	TIME
1-2-3-4	Max Speed 1: _____	
2-1-4	Day 1 @ 30% Max Speed 1: _____	3m
3-2-1	Day 5 @ 30% Max Speed 1: _____	3m
4-3-2	Day 2 @ 80% Max Speed 2: _____	3m
1-4-3	Day 4 @ 90% Max Speed 3: _____	3m
3-1-4	Day 5 @ 90% Max Speed 3: _____	3m
2-3-1	Max Speed 4: _____ Maintenance Level	

DAY 104	Date __ / __ / ____	
EXERCISE PERMUTATION ASCENDING/DESCENDING	EXERCISE DETAIL and METRONOME SPEED SETTING	TIME
2-3-4-1	Max Speed 1: _____	
1-2-3-4	Day 1 @ 30% Max Speed 1: _____	3m
2-1-4	Day 2 @ 30% Max Speed 1: _____	3m
3-2-1	Day 1 @ 50% Max Speed 1: _____	3m
4-3-2	Day 3 @ 80% Max Speed 2: _____	3m
1-4-3	Day 5 @ 90% Max Speed 3: _____	3m
3-1-4	Max Speed 4: _____ Maintenance Level	

DAY 105	Date __ / __ / ____	
EXERCISE PERMUTATION ASCENDING/DESCENDING	EXERCISE DETAIL and METRONOME SPEED SETTING	TIME
3-4-1-2	Max Speed 1: _____	
2-3-4-1	Day 1 @ 30% Max Speed 1: _____	3m
1-2-3-4	Day 2 @ 30% Max Speed 1: _____	3m
2-1-4	Day 3 @ 30% Max Speed 1: _____	3m
3-2-1	Day 2 @ 50% Max Speed 1: _____	3m
4-3-2	Day 4 @ 80% Max Speed 2: _____	3m
1-4-3	Max Speed 4: _____ Maintenance Level	

DAY 106		Date __ / __ / ____
EXERCISE PERMUTATION ASCENDING/DESCENDING	EXERCISE DETAIL and METRONOME SPEED SETTING	TIME
4-1-2-3	Max Speed 1: _____	
3-4-1-2	Day 1 @ 30% Max Speed 1: _____	3m
2-3-4-1	Day 2 @ 30% Max Speed 1: _____	3m
1-2-3-4	Day 3 @ 30% Max Speed 1: _____	3m
2-1-4	Day 4 @ 30% Max Speed 1: _____	3m
3-2-1	Day 3 @ 50% Max Speed 1: _____	3m
4-3-2	Day 5 @ 80% Max Speed 2: _____	3m

DAY 107		Date __ / __ / ____
EXERCISE PERMUTATION ASCENDING/DESCENDING	EXERCISE DETAIL and METRONOME SPEED SETTING	TIME
4-1-2-3	Day 1 @ 30% Max Speed 1: _____	3m
3-4-1-2	Day 2 @ 30% Max Speed 1: _____	3m
2-3-4-1	Day 3 @ 30% Max Speed 1: _____	3m
1-2-3-4	Day 4 @ 30% Max Speed 1: _____	3m
2-1-4	Day 5 @ 30% Max Speed 1: _____	3m
3-2-1	Day 1 @ 65% Max Speed 1: _____	3m
4-3-2	Max Speed 3: _____	

DAY 108		Date __ / __ / ____
EXERCISE PERMUTATION ASCENDING/DESCENDING	EXERCISE DETAIL and METRONOME SPEED SETTING	TIME
4-1-2-3	Day 2 @ 30% Max Speed 1: _____	3m
3-4-1-2	Day 3 @ 30% Max Speed 1: _____	3m
2-3-4-1	Day 4 @ 30% Max Speed 1: _____	3m
1-2-3-4	Day 5 @ 30% Max Speed 1: _____	3m
2-1-4	Day 1 @ 50% Max Speed 1: _____	3m
3-2-1	Day 2 @ 65% Max Speed 1: _____	3m
4-3-2	Day 1 @ 90% Max Speed 3: _____	3m

DAY 109	Date __ / __ / ____	
EXERCISE PERMUTATION ASCENDING/DESCENDING	EXERCISE DETAIL and METRONOME SPEED SETTING	TIME
4-1-2-3	Day 3 @ 30% Max Speed 1: _____	3m
3-4-1-2	Day 4 @ 30% Max Speed 1: _____	3m
2-3-4-1	Day 5 @ 30% Max Speed 1: _____	3m
1-2-3-4	Day 1 @ 50% Max Speed 1: _____	3m
2-1-4	Day 2 @ 50% Max Speed 1: _____	3m
3-2-1	Day 3 @ 65% Max Speed 1: _____	3m
4-3-2	Day 2 @ 90% Max Speed 3: _____	3m

DAY 110	Date __ / __ / ____	
EXERCISE PERMUTATION ASCENDING/DESCENDING	EXERCISE DETAIL and METRONOME SPEED SETTING	TIME
4-1-2-3	Day 4 @ 30% Max Speed 1: _____	3m
3-4-1-2	Day 5 @ 30% Max Speed 1: _____	3m
2-3-4-1	Day 1 @ 50% Max Speed 1: _____	3m
1-2-3-4	Day 2 @ 50% Max Speed 1: _____	3m
2-1-4	Day 3 @ 50% Max Speed 1: _____	3m
3-2-1	Max Speed 2: _____	
4-3-2	Day 3 @ 90% Max Speed 3: _____	3m

DAY 111	Date __ / __ / ____	
EXERCISE PERMUTATION ASCENDING/DESCENDING	EXERCISE DETAIL and METRONOME SPEED SETTING	TIME
4-1-2-3	Day 5 @ 30% Max Speed 1: _____	3m
3-4-1-2	Day 1 @ 50% Max Speed 1: _____	3m
2-3-4-1	Day 2 @ 50% Max Speed 1: _____	3m
1-2-3-4	Day 3 @ 50% Max Speed 1: _____	3m
2-1-4	Day 1 @ 65% Max Speed 1: _____	3m
3-2-1	Day 1 @ 80% Max Speed 2: _____	3m
4-3-2	Day 4 @ 90% Max Speed 3: _____	3m

DAY 112		Date __ /__ /____
EXERCISE PERMUTATION ASCENDING/DESCENDING	EXERCISE DETAIL and METRONOME SPEED SETTING	TIME
4-1-2-3	Day 1 @ 50% Max Speed 1: _____	3m
3-4-1-2	Day 2 @ 50% Max Speed 1: _____	3m
2-3-4-1	Day 3 @ 50% Max Speed 1: _____	3m
1-2-3-4	Day 1 @ 65% Max Speed 1: _____	3m
2-1-4	Day 2 @ 65% Max Speed 1: _____	3m
3-2-1	Day 2 @ 80% Max Speed 2: _____	3m
4-3-2	Day 5 @ 90% Max Speed 3: _____	3m

DAY 113		Date __ /__ /____
EXERCISE PERMUTATION ASCENDING/DESCENDING	EXERCISE DETAIL and METRONOME SPEED SETTING	TIME
4-1-2-3	Day 2 @ 50% Max Speed 1: _____	3m
3-4-1-2	Day 3 @ 50% Max Speed 1: _____	3m
2-3-4-1	Day 1 @ 65% Max Speed 1: _____	3m
1-2-3-4	Day 2 @ 65% Max Speed 1: _____	3m
2-1-4	Day 3 @ 65% Max Speed 1: _____	3m
3-2-1	Day 3 @ 80% Max Speed 2: _____	3m
4-3-2	Max Speed 4: _____ Maintenance Level	

DAY 114		Date __ /__ /____
EXERCISE PERMUTATION ASCENDING/DESCENDING	EXERCISE DETAIL and METRONOME SPEED SETTING	TIME
1-2-4-3	Max Speed 1: _____	
4-1-2-3	Day 3 @ 50% Max Speed 1: _____	3m
3-4-1-2	Day 1 @ 65% Max Speed 1: _____	3m
2-3-4-1	Day 2 @ 65% Max Speed 1: _____	3m
1-2-3-4	Day 3 @ 65% Max Speed 1: _____	3m
2-1-4	Max Speed 2: _____	
3-2-1	Day 4 @ 80% Max Speed 2: _____	3m

DAY 115	Date __ / __ / ____	
EXERCISE PERMUTATION ASCENDING/DESCENDING	EXERCISE DETAIL and METRONOME SPEED SETTING	TIME
1-2-4-3	Day 1 @ 30% Max Speed 1: _____	3m
4-1-2-3	Day 1 @ 65% Max Speed 1: _____	3m
3-4-1-2	Day 2 @ 65% Max Speed 1: _____	3m
2-3-4-1	Day 3 @ 65% Max Speed 1: _____	3m
1-2-3-4	Max Speed 2: _____	
2-1-4	Day 1 @ 80% Max Speed 2: _____	3m
3-2-1	Day 5 @ 80% Max Speed 2: _____	3m

DAY 116	Date __ / __ / ____	
EXERCISE PERMUTATION ASCENDING/DESCENDING	EXERCISE DETAIL and METRONOME SPEED SETTING	TIME
1-2-4-3	Day 2 @ 30% Max Speed 1: _____	3m
4-1-2-3	Day 2 @ 65% Max Speed 1: _____	3m
3-4-1-2	Day 3 @ 65% Max Speed 1: _____	3m
2-3-4-1	Max Speed 2: _____	
1-2-3-4	Day 1 @ 80% Max Speed 2: _____	3m
2-1-4	Day 2 @ 80% Max Speed 2: _____	3m
3-2-1	Max Speed 3: _____	

DAY 117	Date __ / __ / ____	
EXERCISE PERMUTATION ASCENDING/DESCENDING	EXERCISE DETAIL and METRONOME SPEED SETTING	TIME
1-2-4-3	Day 3 @ 30% Max Speed 1: _____	3m
4-1-2-3	Day 3 @ 65% Max Speed 1: _____	3m
3-4-1-2	Max Speed 2: _____	
2-3-4-1	Day 1 @ 80% Max Speed 2: _____	3m
1-2-3-4	Day 2 @ 80% Max Speed 2: _____	3m
2-1-4	Day 3 @ 80% Max Speed 2: _____	3m
3-2-1	Day 1 @ 90% Max Speed 3: _____	3m

DAY 118		Date __ / __ / ____
EXERCISE PERMUTATION ASCENDING/DESCENDING	EXERCISE DETAIL and METRONOME SPEED SETTING	TIME
1-2-4-3	Day 4 @ 30% Max Speed 1: _____	3m
4-1-2-3	Max Speed 2: _____	
3-4-1-2	Day 1 @ 80% Max Speed 2: _____	3m
2-3-4-1	Day 2 @ 80% Max Speed 2: _____	3m
1-2-3-4	Day 3 @ 80% Max Speed 2: _____	3m
2-1-4	Day 4 @ 80% Max Speed 2: _____	3m
3-2-1	Day 2 @ 90% Max Speed 3: _____	3m

DAY 119		Date __ / __ / ____
EXERCISE PERMUTATION ASCENDING/DESCENDING	EXERCISE DETAIL and METRONOME SPEED SETTING	TIME
1-2-4-3	Day 5 @ 30% Max Speed 1: _____	3m
4-1-2-3	Day 1 @ 80% Max Speed 2: _____	3m
3-4-1-2	Day 2 @ 80% Max Speed 2: _____	3m
2-3-4-1	Day 3 @ 80% Max Speed 2: _____	3m
1-2-3-4	Day 4 @ 80% Max Speed 2: _____	3m
2-1-4	Day 5 @ 80% Max Speed 2: _____	3m
3-2-1	Day 3 @ 90% Max Speed 3: _____	3m

DAY 120		Date __ / __ / ____
EXERCISE PERMUTATION ASCENDING/DESCENDING	EXERCISE DETAIL and METRONOME SPEED SETTING	TIME
1-2-4-3	Day 1 @ 50% Max Speed 1: _____	3m
4-1-2-3	Day 2 @ 80% Max Speed 2: _____	3m
3-4-1-2	Day 3 @ 80% Max Speed 2: _____	3m
2-3-4-1	Day 4 @ 80% Max Speed 2: _____	3m
1-2-3-4	Day 5 @ 80% Max Speed 2: _____	3m
2-1-4	Max Speed 3: _____	
3-2-1	Day 4 @ 90% Max Speed 3: _____	3m

DAY 121	Date __ / __ / ____	
EXERCISE PERMUTATION ASCENDING/DESCENDING	EXERCISE DETAIL and METRONOME SPEED SETTING	TIME
1-2-4-3	Day 2 @ 50% Max Speed 1: _____	3m
4-1-2-3	Day 3 @ 80% Max Speed 2: _____	3m
3-4-1-2	Day 4 @ 80% Max Speed 2: _____	3m
2-3-4-1	Day 5 @ 80% Max Speed 2: _____	3m
1-2-3-4	Max Speed 3: _____	
2-1-4	Day 1 @ 90% Max Speed 3: _____	3m
3-2-1	Day 5 @ 90% Max Speed 3: _____	3m

DAY 122	Date __ / __ / ____	
EXERCISE PERMUTATION ASCENDING/DESCENDING	EXERCISE DETAIL and METRONOME SPEED SETTING	TIME
1-2-4-3	Day 3 @ 50% Max Speed 1: _____	3m
4-1-2-3	Day 4 @ 80% Max Speed 2: _____	3m
3-4-1-2	Day 5 @ 80% Max Speed 2: _____	3m
2-3-4-1	Max Speed 3: _____	
1-2-3-4	Day 1 @ 90% Max Speed 3: _____	3m
2-1-4	Day 2 @ 90% Max Speed 3: _____	3m
3-2-1	Max Speed 4: _____ Maintenance Level	

DAY 123	Date __ / __ / ____	
EXERCISE PERMUTATION ASCENDING/DESCENDING	EXERCISE DETAIL and METRONOME SPEED SETTING	TIME
2-4-3-1	Max Speed 1: _____	
1-2-4-3	Day 3 @ 50% Max Speed 1: _____	3m
4-1-2-3	Day 5 @ 80% Max Speed 2: _____	3m
3-4-1-2	Max Speed 3: _____	
2-3-4-1	Day 1 @ 90% Max Speed 3: _____	3m
1-2-3-4	Day 2 @ 90% Max Speed 3: _____	3m
2-1-4	Day 3 @ 90% Max Speed 3: _____	3m

DAY 124	Date __ / __ / ____	
EXERCISE PERMUTATION ASCENDING/DESCENDING	EXERCISE DETAIL and METRONOME SPEED SETTING	TIME
2-4-3-1	Day 1 @ 30% Max Speed 1: _____	3m
1-2-4-3	Day 1 @ 65% Max Speed 1: _____	3m
4-1-2-3	Max Speed 3: _____	
3-4-1-2	Day 1 @ 90% Max Speed 3: _____	3m
2-3-4-1	Day 2 @ 90% Max Speed 3: _____	3m
1-2-3-4	Day 3 @ 90% Max Speed 3: _____	3m
2-1-4	Day 4 @ 90% Max Speed 3: _____	3m

DAY 125	Date __ / __ / ____	
EXERCISE PERMUTATION ASCENDING/DESCENDING	EXERCISE DETAIL and METRONOME SPEED SETTING	TIME
2-4-3-1	Day 2 @ 30% Max Speed 1: _____	3m
1-2-4-3	Day 2 @ 65% Max Speed 1: _____	3m
4-1-2-3	Day 1 @ 90% Max Speed 3: _____	
3-4-1-2	Day 2 @ 90% Max Speed 3: _____	3m
2-3-4-1	Day 3 @ 90% Max Speed 3: _____	3m
1-2-3-4	Day 4 @ 90% Max Speed 3: _____	3m
2-1-4	Day 5 @ 90% Max Speed 3: _____	3m

DAY 126	Date __ / __ / ____	
EXERCISE PERMUTATION ASCENDING/DESCENDING	EXERCISE DETAIL and METRONOME SPEED SETTING	TIME
2-4-3-1	Day 3 @ 30% Max Speed 1: _____	3m
1-2-4-3	Day 3 @ 65% Max Speed 1: _____	3m
4-1-2-3	Day 2 @ 90% Max Speed 3: _____	3m
3-4-1-2	Day 3 @ 90% Max Speed 3: _____	3m
2-3-4-1	Day 4 @ 90% Max Speed 3: _____	3m
1-2-3-4	Day 5 @ 90% Max Speed 3: _____	3m
2-1-4	Max Speed 4: _____ Maintenance Level	

DAY 127	Date __ /__ /____	
EXERCISE PERMUTATION ASCENDING/DESCENDING	EXERCISE DETAIL and METRONOME SPEED SETTING	TIME
4-3-1-2	Max Speed 1: _____	
2-4-3-1	Day 4 @ 30% Max Speed 1: _____	3m
1-2-4-3	Max Speed 2: _____	
4-1-2-3	Day 3 @ 90% Max Speed 3: _____	3m
3-4-1-2	Day 4 @ 90% Max Speed 3: _____	3m
2-3-4-1	Day 5 @ 90% Max Speed 3: _____	3m
1-2-3-4	Max Speed 4: _____ Maintenance Level	

DAY 128	Date __ /__ /____	
EXERCISE PERMUTATION ASCENDING/DESCENDING	EXERCISE DETAIL and METRONOME SPEED SETTING	TIME
3-1-2-4	Max Speed 1: _____	
4-3-1-2	Day 1 @ 30% Max Speed 1: _____	3m
2-4-3-1	Day 5 @ 30% Max Speed 1: _____	3m
1-2-4-3	Day 1 @ 80% Max Speed 2: _____	3m
4-1-2-3	Day 4 @ 90% Max Speed 3: _____	3m
3-4-1-2	Day 5 @ 90% Max Speed 3: _____	3m
2-3-4-1	Max Speed 4: _____ Maintenance Level	

DAY 129	Date __ /__ /____	
EXERCISE PERMUTATION ASCENDING/DESCENDING	EXERCISE DETAIL and METRONOME SPEED SETTING	TIME
1-3-2-4	Max Speed 1: _____	
3-1-2-4	Day 1 @ 30% Max Speed 1: _____	3m
4-3-1-2	Day 2 @ 30% Max Speed 1: _____	3m
2-4-3-1	Day 1 @ 50% Max Speed 1: _____	3m
1-2-4-3	Day 2 @ 80% Max Speed 2: _____	3m
4-1-2-3	Day 5 @ 90% Max Speed 3: _____	3m
3-4-1-2	Max Speed 4: _____ Maintenance Level	

DAY 130	Date __/__/____	
EXERCISE PERMUTATION ASCENDING/DESCENDING	EXERCISE DETAIL and METRONOME SPEED SETTING	TIME
3-2-4-1	Max Speed 1: _____	
1-3-2-4	Day 1 @ 30% Max Speed 1: _____	3m
3-1-2-4	Day 2 @ 30% Max Speed 1: _____	3m
4-3-1-2	Day 3 @ 30% Max Speed 1: _____	3m
2-4-3-1	Day 2 @ 50% Max Speed 1: _____	3m
1-2-4-3	Day 3 @ 80% Max Speed 2: _____	3m
4-1-2-3	Max Speed 4: _____ Maintenance Level	

DAY 131	Date __/__/____	
EXERCISE PERMUTATION ASCENDING/DESCENDING	EXERCISE DETAIL and METRONOME SPEED SETTING	TIME
2-4-1-3	Max Speed 1: _____	
3-2-4-1	Day 1 @ 30% Max Speed 1: _____	3m
1-3-2-4	Day 2 @ 30% Max Speed 1: _____	3m
3-1-2-4	Day 3 @ 30% Max Speed 1: _____	3m
4-3-1-2	Day 4 @ 30% Max Speed 1: _____	3m
2-4-3-1	Day 3 @ 50% Max Speed 1: _____	3m
1-2-4-3	Day 4 @ 80% Max Speed 2: _____	3m

DAY 132	Date __/__/____	
EXERCISE PERMUTATION ASCENDING/DESCENDING	EXERCISE DETAIL and METRONOME SPEED SETTING	TIME
2-4-1-3	Day 1 @ 30% Max Speed 1: _____	3m
3-2-4-1	Day 2 @ 30% Max Speed 1: _____	3m
1-3-2-4	Day 3 @ 30% Max Speed 1: _____	3m
3-1-2-4	Day 4 @ 30% Max Speed 1: _____	3m
4-3-1-2	Day 5 @ 30% Max Speed 1: _____	3m
2-4-3-1	Day 1 @ 65% Max Speed 1: _____	3m
1-2-4-3	Day 5 @ 80% Max Speed 2: _____	3m

DAY 133	Date __ / __ / ____	
EXERCISE PERMUTATION ASCENDING/DESCENDING	EXERCISE DETAIL and METRONOME SPEED SETTING	TIME
2-4-1-3	Day 2 @ 30% Max Speed 1: _____	3m
3-2-4-1	Day 3 @ 30% Max Speed 1: _____	3m
1-3-2-4	Day 4 @ 30% Max Speed 1: _____	3m
3-1-2-4	Day 5 @ 30% Max Speed 1: _____	3m
4-3-1-2	Day 1 @ 50% Max Speed 1: _____	3m
2-4-3-1	Day 2 @ 65% Max Speed 1: _____	3m
1-2-4-3	Max Speed 3: _____	

DAY 134	Date __ / __ / ____	
EXERCISE PERMUTATION ASCENDING/DESCENDING	EXERCISE DETAIL and METRONOME SPEED SETTING	TIME
2-4-1-3	Day 3 @ 30% Max Speed 1: _____	3m
3-2-4-1	Day 4 @ 30% Max Speed 1: _____	3m
1-3-2-4	Day 5 @ 30% Max Speed 1: _____	3m
3-1-2-4	Day 1 @ 50% Max Speed 1: _____	3m
4-3-1-2	Day 2 @ 50% Max Speed 1: _____	3m
2-4-3-1	Day 3 @ 65% Max Speed 1: _____	3m
1-2-4-3	Day 1 @ 90% Max Speed 3: _____	3m

DAY 135	Date __ / __ / ____	
EXERCISE PERMUTATION ASCENDING/DESCENDING	EXERCISE DETAIL and METRONOME SPEED SETTING	TIME
2-4-1-3	Day 4 @ 30% Max Speed 1: _____	3m
3-2-4-1	Day 5 @ 30% Max Speed 1: _____	3m
1-3-2-4	Day 1 @ 50% Max Speed 1: _____	3m
3-1-2-4	Day 2 @ 50% Max Speed 1: _____	3m
4-3-1-2	Day 3 @ 50% Max Speed 1: _____	3m
2-4-3-1	Max Speed 2: _____	3m
1-2-4-3	Day 2 @ 90% Max Speed 3: _____	3m

DAY 136	Date __ / __ / ____	
EXERCISE PERMUTATION ASCENDING/DESCENDING	EXERCISE DETAIL and METRONOME SPEED SETTING	TIME
2-4-1-3	Day 5 @ 30% Max Speed 1: _____	3m
3-2-4-1	Day 1 @ 50% Max Speed 1: _____	3m
1-3-2-4	Day 2 @ 50% Max Speed 1: _____	3m
3-1-2-4	Day 3 @ 50% Max Speed 1: _____	3m
4-3-1-2	Day 1 @ 65% Max Speed 1: _____	3m
2-4-3-1	Day 1 @ 80% Max Speed 2: _____	3m
1-2-4-3	Day 3 @ 90% Max Speed 3: _____	3m

DAY 137	Date __ / __ / ____	
EXERCISE PERMUTATION ASCENDING/DESCENDING	EXERCISE DETAIL and METRONOME SPEED SETTING	TIME
2-4-1-3	Day 1 @ 50% Max Speed 1: _____	3m
3-2-4-1	Day 2 @ 50% Max Speed 1: _____	3m
1-3-2-4	Day 3 @ 50% Max Speed 1: _____	3m
3-1-2-4	Day 1 @ 65% Max Speed 1: _____	3m
4-3-1-2	Day 2 @ 65% Max Speed 1: _____	3m
2-4-3-1	Day 2 @ 80% Max Speed 2: _____	3m
1-2-4-3	Day 4 @ 90% Max Speed 3: _____	3m

DAY 138	Date __ / __ / ____	
EXERCISE PERMUTATION ASCENDING/DESCENDING	EXERCISE DETAIL and METRONOME SPEED SETTING	TIME
2-4-1-3	Day 2 @ 50% Max Speed 1: _____	3m
3-2-4-1	Day 3 @ 50% Max Speed 1: _____	3m
1-3-2-4	Day 1 @ 65% Max Speed 1: _____	3m
3-1-2-4	Day 2 @ 65% Max Speed 1: _____	3m
4-3-1-2	Day 3 @ 65% Max Speed 1: _____	3m
2-4-3-1	Day 3 @ 80% Max Speed 2: _____	3m
1-2-4-3	Day 5 @ 90% Max Speed 3: _____	3m

DAY 139	Date __ / __ / ____	
EXERCISE PERMUTATION ASCENDING/DESCENDING	EXERCISE DETAIL and METRONOME SPEED SETTING	TIME
2-4-1-3	Day 3 @ 50% Max Speed 1: _____	3m
3-2-4-1	Day 1 @ 65% Max Speed 1: _____	3m
1-3-2-4	Day 2 @ 65% Max Speed 1: _____	3m
3-1-2-4	Day 3 @ 65% Max Speed 1: _____	3m
4-3-1-2	Max Speed 2: _____	
2-4-3-1	Day 4 @ 80% Max Speed 2: _____	3m
1-2-4-3	Max Speed 4 : _____ Maintenance Level	

DAY 140	Date __ / __ / ____	
EXERCISE PERMUTATION ASCENDING/DESCENDING	EXERCISE DETAIL and METRONOME SPEED SETTING	TIME
4-1-3-2	Max Speed 1: _____	
2-4-1-3	Day 1 @ 65% Max Speed 1: _____	3m
3-2-4-1	Day 2 @ 65% Max Speed 1: _____	3m
1-3-2-4	Day 3 @ 65% Max Speed 1: _____	3m
3-1-2-4	Max Speed 2: _____	
4-3-1-2	Day 1 @ 80% Max Speed 2: _____	3m
2-4-3-1	Day 4 @ 80% Max Speed 2: _____	3m

DAY 141	Date __ / __ / ____	
EXERCISE PERMUTATION ASCENDING/DESCENDING	EXERCISE DETAIL and METRONOME SPEED SETTING	TIME
4-1-3-2	Day 1 @ 30% Max Speed 1: _____	3m
2-4-1-3	Day 2 @ 65% Max Speed 1: _____	3m
3-2-4-1	Day 3 @ 65% Max Speed 1: _____	3m
1-3-2-4	Max Speed 2: _____	
3-1-2-4	Day 1 @ 80% Max Speed 2: _____	3m
4-3-1-2	Day 2 @ 80% Max Speed 2: _____	3m
2-4-3-1	Day 5 @ 80% Max Speed 2: _____	3m

DAY 142		Date __ / __ / ____
EXERCISE PERMUTATION ASCENDING/DESCENDING	EXERCISE DETAIL and METRONOME SPEED SETTING	TIME
4-1-3-2	Day 2 @ 30% Max Speed 1: _____	3m
2-4-1-3	Day 3 @ 65% Max Speed 1: _____	3m
3-2-4-1	Max Speed 2: _____	
1-3-2-4	Day 1 @ 80% Max Speed 2: _____	3m
3-1-2-4	Day 2 @ 80% Max Speed 2: _____	3m
4-3-1-2	Day 3 @ 80% Max Speed 2: _____	3m
2-4-3-1	Max Speed 3: _____	3m

DAY 143		Date __ / __ / ____
EXERCISE PERMUTATION ASCENDING/DESCENDING	EXERCISE DETAIL and METRONOME SPEED SETTING	TIME
4-1-3-2	Day 3 @ 30% Max Speed 1: _____	3m
2-4-1-3	Max Speed 2: _____	
3-2-4-1	Day 1 @ 80% Max Speed 2: _____	3m
1-3-2-4	Day 2 @ 80% Max Speed 2: _____	3m
3-1-2-4	Day 3 @ 80% Max Speed 2: _____	3m
4-3-1-2	Day 4 @ 80% Max Speed 2: _____	3m
2-4-3-1	Day 1 @ 90% Max Speed 3: _____	3m

DAY 144		Date __ / __ / ____
EXERCISE PERMUTATION ASCENDING/DESCENDING	EXERCISE DETAIL and METRONOME SPEED SETTING	TIME
4-1-3-2	Day 4 @ 30% Max Speed 1: _____	3m
2-4-1-3	Day 1 @ 80% Max Speed 2: _____	3m
3-2-4-1	Day 2 @ 80% Max Speed 2: _____	3m
1-3-2-4	Day 3 @ 80% Max Speed 2: _____	3m
3-1-2-4	Day 4 @ 80% Max Speed 2: _____	3m
4-3-1-2	Day 5 @ 80% Max Speed 2: _____	3m
2-4-3-1	Day 2 @ 90% Max Speed 3: _____	3m

DAY 145	Date __/__/____	
EXERCISE PERMUTATION ASCENDING/DESCENDING	EXERCISE DETAIL and METRONOME SPEED SETTING	TIME
4-1-3-2	Day 5 @ 30% Max Speed 1: _____	3m
2-4-1-3	Day 2 @ 80% Max Speed 2: _____	3m
3-2-4-1	Day 3 @ 80% Max Speed 2: _____	3m
1-3-2-4	Day 4 @ 80% Max Speed 2: _____	3m
3-1-2-4	Day 5 @ 80% Max Speed 2: _____	3m
4-3-1-2	Max Speed 3: _____	
2-4-3-1	Day 3 @ 90% Max Speed 3: _____	3m

DAY 146	Date __/__/____	
EXERCISE PERMUTATION ASCENDING/DESCENDING	EXERCISE DETAIL and METRONOME SPEED SETTING	TIME
4-1-3-2	Day 1 @ 50% Max Speed 1: _____	3m
2-4-1-3	Day 3 @ 80% Max Speed 2: _____	3m
3-2-4-1	Day 4 @ 80% Max Speed 2: _____	3m
1-3-2-4	Day 5 @ 80% Max Speed 2: _____	3m
3-1-2-4	Max Speed 3: _____	
4-3-1-2	Day 1 @ 90% Max Speed 3: _____	3m
2-4-3-1	Day 4 @ 90% Max Speed 3: _____	3m

DAY 147	Date __/__/____	
EXERCISE PERMUTATION ASCENDING/DESCENDING	EXERCISE DETAIL and METRONOME SPEED SETTING	TIME
4-1-3-2	Day 2 @ 50% Max Speed 1: _____	3m
2-4-1-3	Day 4 @ 80% Max Speed 2: _____	3m
3-2-4-1	Day 5 @ 80% Max Speed 2: _____	3m
1-3-2-4	Max Speed 3: _____	
3-1-2-4	Day 1 @ 90% Max Speed 3: _____	3m
4-3-1-2	Day 2 @ 90% Max Speed 3: _____	3m
2-4-3-1	Day 5 @ 90% Max Speed 3: _____	3m

DAY 148	Date __ / __ / ____	
EXERCISE PERMUTATION ASCENDING/DESCENDING	EXERCISE DETAIL and METRONOME SPEED SETTING	TIME
4-1-3-2	Day 3 @ 50% Max Speed 1: _____	3m
2-4-1-3	Day 5 @ 80% Max Speed 2: _____	3m
3-2-4-1	Max Speed 3: _____	
1-3-2-4	Day 1 @ 90% Max Speed 3: _____	3m
3-1-2-4	Day 2 @ 90% Max Speed 3: _____	3m
4-3-1-2	Day 3 @ 90% Max Speed 3: _____	3m
2-4-3-1	Max Speed 4: _____ Maintenance Level	

DAY 149	Date __ / __ / ____	
EXERCISE PERMUTATION ASCENDING/DESCENDING	EXERCISE DETAIL and METRONOME SPEED SETTING	TIME
1-3-4-2	Max Speed 1: _____	
4-1-3-2	Day 1 @ 65% Max Speed 1: _____	3m
2-4-1-3	Max Speed 3: _____	
3-2-4-1	Day 1 @ 90% Max Speed 3: _____	3m
1-3-2-4	Day 2 @ 90% Max Speed 3: _____	3m
3-1-2-4	Day 3 @ 90% Max Speed 3: _____	3m
4-3-1-2	Day 4 @ 90% Max Speed 3: _____	3m

DAY 150	Date __ / __ / ____	
EXERCISE PERMUTATION ASCENDING/DESCENDING	EXERCISE DETAIL and METRONOME SPEED SETTING	TIME
1-3-4-2	Day 1 @ 30% Max Speed 1: _____	3m
4-1-3-2	Day 2 @ 65% Max Speed 1: _____	3m
2-4-1-3	Day 1 @ 90% Max Speed 3: _____	3m
3-2-4-1	Day 2 @ 90% Max Speed 3: _____	3m
1-3-2-4	Day 3 @ 90% Max Speed 3: _____	3m
3-1-2-4	Day 4 @ 90% Max Speed 3: _____	3m
4-3-1-2	Day 5 @ 90% Max Speed 3: _____	3m

DAY 151	Date __ / __ / ____	
EXERCISE PERMUTATION ASCENDING/DESCENDING	EXERCISE DETAIL and METRONOME SPEED SETTING	TIME
1-3-4-2	Day 2 @ 30% Max Speed 1: _____	3m
4-1-3-2	Day 3 @ 65% Max Speed 1: _____	3m
2-4-1-3	Day 2 @ 90% Max Speed 3: _____	3m
3-2-4-1	Day 3 @ 90% Max Speed 3: _____	3m
1-3-2-4	Day 4 @ 90% Max Speed 3: _____	3m
3-1-2-4	Day 5 @ 90% Max Speed 3: _____	3m
4-3-1-2	Max Speed 4: _____ Maintenance Level	

DAY 152	Date __ / __ / ____	
EXERCISE PERMUTATION ASCENDING/DESCENDING	EXERCISE DETAIL and METRONOME SPEED SETTING	TIME
3-4-2-1	Max Speed 1: _____	
1-3-4-2	Day 3 @ 30% Max Speed 1: _____	3m
4-1-3-2	Max Speed 2: _____	
2-4-1-3	Day 3 @ 90% Max Speed 3: _____	3m
3-2-4-1	Day 4 @ 90% Max Speed 3: _____	3m
1-3-2-4	Day 5 @ 90% Max Speed 3: _____	3m
3-1-2-4	Max Speed 4: _____ Maintenance Level	

DAY 153	Date __ / __ / ____	
EXERCISE PERMUTATION ASCENDING/DESCENDING	EXERCISE DETAIL and METRONOME SPEED SETTING	TIME
4-2-1-3	Max Speed 1: _____	
3-4-2-1	Day 1 @ 30% Max Speed 1: _____	3m
1-3-4-2	Day 4 @ 30% Max Speed 1: _____	3m
4-1-3-2	Day 1 @ 80% Max Speed 2: _____	3m
2-4-1-3	Day 4 @ 90% Max Speed 3: _____	3m
3-2-4-1	Day 5 @ 90% Max Speed 3: _____	3m
1-3-2-4	Max Speed 4: _____ Maintenance Level	

DAY 154		Date __ / __ / ____
EXERCISE PERMUTATION ASCENDING/DESCENDING	EXERCISE DETAIL and METRONOME SPEED SETTING	TIME
2-1-3-4	Max Speed 1: _____	
4-2-1-3	Day 1 @ 30% Max Speed 1: _____	3m
3-4-2-1	Day 2 @ 30% Max Speed 1: _____	3m
1-3-4-2	Day 5 @ 30% Max Speed 1: _____	3m
4-1-3-2	Day 2 @ 80% Max Speed 2: _____	3m
2-4-1-3	Day 5 @ 90% Max Speed 3: _____	3m
3-2-4-1	Max Speed 4: _____ Maintenance Level	

DAY 155		Date __ / __ / ____
EXERCISE PERMUTATION ASCENDING/DESCENDING	EXERCISE DETAIL and METRONOME SPEED SETTING	TIME
1-4-2-3	Max Speed 1: _____	
2-1-3-4	Day 1 @ 30% Max Speed 1: _____	3m
4-2-1-3	Day 2 @ 30% Max Speed 1: _____	3m
3-4-2-1	Day 3 @ 30% Max Speed 1: _____	3m
1-3-4-2	Day 1 @ 50% Max Speed 1: _____	3m
4-1-3-2	Day 3 @ 80% Max Speed 2: _____	3m
2-4-1-3	Max Speed 4: _____ Maintenance Level	

DAY 156		Date __ / __ / ____
EXERCISE PERMUTATION ASCENDING/DESCENDING	EXERCISE DETAIL and METRONOME SPEED SETTING	TIME
4-2-3-1	Max Speed 1: _____	
1-4-2-3	Day 1 @ 30% Max Speed 1: _____	3m
2-1-3-4	Day 2 @ 30% Max Speed 1: _____	3m
4-2-1-3	Day 3 @ 30% Max Speed 1: _____	3m
3-4-2-1	Day 4 @ 30% Max Speed 1: _____	3m
1-3-4-2	Day 2 @ 50% Max Speed 1: _____	3m
4-1-3-2	Day 4 @ 80% Max Speed 2: _____	3m

DAY 157	Date __ / __ / ____	
EXERCISE PERMUTATION ASCENDING/DESCENDING	**EXERCISE DETAIL and METRONOME SPEED SETTING**	**TIME**
4-2-3-1	Day 1 @ 30% Max Speed 1: _____	3m
1-4-2-3	Day 2 @ 30% Max Speed 1: _____	3m
2-1-3-4	Day 3 @ 30% Max Speed 1: _____	3m
4-2-1-3	Day 4 @ 30% Max Speed 1: _____	3m
3-4-2-1	Day 5 @ 30% Max Speed 1: _____	3m
1-3-4-2	Day 3 @ 50% Max Speed 1: _____	3m
4-1-3-2	Day 5 @ 80% Max Speed 2: _____	3m

DAY 158	Date __ / __ / ____	
EXERCISE PERMUTATION ASCENDING/DESCENDING	**EXERCISE DETAIL and METRONOME SPEED SETTING**	**TIME**
4-2-3-1	Day 2 @ 30% Max Speed 1: _____	3m
1-4-2-3	Day 3 @ 30% Max Speed 1: _____	3m
2-1-3-4	Day 4 @ 30% Max Speed 1: _____	3m
4-2-1-3	Day 5 @ 30% Max Speed 1: _____	3m
3-4-2-1	Day 1 @ 50% Max Speed 1: _____	3m
1-3-4-2	Day 1 @ 65% Max Speed 1: _____	3m
4-1-3-2	Max Speed 3: _____	

DAY 159	Date __ / __ / ____	
EXERCISE PERMUTATION ASCENDING/DESCENDING	**EXERCISE DETAIL and METRONOME SPEED SETTING**	**TIME**
4-2-3-1	Day 3 @ 30% Max Speed 1: _____	3m
1-4-2-3	Day 4 @ 30% Max Speed 1: _____	3m
2-1-3-4	Day 5 @ 30% Max Speed 1: _____	3m
4-2-1-3	Day 1 @ 50% Max Speed 1: _____	3m
3-4-2-1	Day 2 @ 50% Max Speed 1: _____	3m
1-3-4-2	Day 2 @ 65% Max Speed 1: _____	3m
4-1-3-2	Day 1 @ 90% Max Speed 3: _____	3m

DAY 160	Date __ / __ / ____	
EXERCISE PERMUTATION ASCENDING/DESCENDING	EXERCISE DETAIL and METRONOME SPEED SETTING	TIME
4-2-3-1	Day 4 @ 30% Max Speed 1: _____	3m
1-4-2-3	Day 5 @ 30% Max Speed 1: _____	3m
2-1-3-4	Day 1 @ 50% Max Speed 1: _____	3m
4-2-1-3	Day 2 @ 50% Max Speed 1: _____	3m
3-4-2-1	Day 3 @ 50% Max Speed 1: _____	3m
1-3-4-2	Day 3 @ 65% Max Speed 1: _____	3m
4-1-3-2	Day 2 @ 90% Max Speed 3: _____	3m

DAY 161	Date __ / __ / ____	
EXERCISE PERMUTATION ASCENDING/DESCENDING	EXERCISE DETAIL and METRONOME SPEED SETTING	TIME
4-2-3-1	Day 5 @ 30% Max Speed 1: _____	3m
1-4-2-3	Day 1 @ 50% Max Speed 1: _____	3m
2-1-3-4	Day 2 @ 50% Max Speed 1: _____	3m
4-2-1-3	Day 3 @ 50% Max Speed 1: _____	3m
3-4-2-1	Day 1 @ 65% Max Speed 1: _____	3m
1-3-4-2	Max Speed 2: _____	
4-1-3-2	Day 3 @ 90% Max Speed 3: _____	3m

DAY 162	Date __ / __ / ____	
EXERCISE PERMUTATION ASCENDING/DESCENDING	EXERCISE DETAIL and METRONOME SPEED SETTING	TIME
4-2-3-1	Day 1 @ 50% Max Speed 1: _____	3m
1-4-2-3	Day 2 @ 50% Max Speed 1: _____	3m
2-1-3-4	Day 3 @ 50% Max Speed 1: _____	3m
4-2-1-3	Day 1 @ 65% Max Speed 1: _____	3m
3-4-2-1	Day 2 @ 65% Max Speed 1: _____	3m
1-3-4-2	Day 1 @ 80% Max Speed 2: _____	3m
4-1-3-2	Day 4 @ 90% Max Speed 3: _____	3m

DAY 163	Date __ / __ / ____	
EXERCISE PERMUTATION ASCENDING/DESCENDING	EXERCISE DETAIL and METRONOME SPEED SETTING	TIME
4-2-3-1	Day 2 @ 50% Max Speed 1: _____	3m
1-4-2-3	Day 3 @ 50% Max Speed 1: _____	3m
2-1-3-4	Day 1 @ 65% Max Speed 1: _____	3m
4-2-1-3	Day 2 @ 65% Max Speed 1: _____	3m
3-4-2-1	Day 3 @ 65% Max Speed 1: _____	3m
1-3-4-2	Day 2 @ 80% Max Speed 2: _____	3m
4-1-3-2	Day 5 @ 90% Max Speed 3: _____	3m

DAY 164	Date __ / __ / ____	
EXERCISE PERMUTATION ASCENDING/DESCENDING	EXERCISE DETAIL and METRONOME SPEED SETTING	TIME
4-2-3-1	Day 3 @ 50% Max Speed 1: _____	3m
1-4-2-3	Day 1 @ 65% Max Speed 1: _____	3m
2-1-3-4	Day 2 @ 65% Max Speed 1: _____	3m
4-2-1-3	Day 3 @ 65% Max Speed 1: _____	3m
3-4-2-1	Max Speed 2: _____	
1-3-4-2	Day 3 @ 80% Max Speed 2: _____	3m
4-1-3-2	Max Speed 4: _____ Maintenance Level	

DAY 165	Date __ / __ / ____	
EXERCISE PERMUTATION ASCENDING/DESCENDING	EXERCISE DETAIL and METRONOME SPEED SETTING	TIME
2-3-1-4	Max Speed 1: _____	
4-2-3-1	Day 1 @ 65% Max Speed 1: _____	3m
1-4-2-3	Day 2 @ 65% Max Speed 1: _____	3m
2-1-3-4	Day 3 @ 65% Max Speed 1: _____	3m
4-2-1-3	Max Speed 2: _____	
3-4-2-1	Day 1 @ 80% Max Speed 2: _____	3m
1-3-4-2	Day 4 @ 80% Max Speed 2: _____	3m

DAY 166	Date __ / __ / ____	
EXERCISE PERMUTATION ASCENDING/DESCENDING	EXERCISE DETAIL and METRONOME SPEED SETTING	TIME
2-3-1-4	Day 1 @ 30% Max Speed 1: _____	3m
4-2-3-1	Day 2 @ 65% Max Speed 1: _____	3m
1-4-2-3	Day 3 @ 65% Max Speed 1: _____	3m
2-1-3-4	Max Speed 2: _____	
4-2-1-3	Day 1 @ 80% Max Speed 2: _____	3m
3-4-2-1	Day 2 @ 80% Max Speed 2: _____	3m
1-3-4-2	Day 5 @ 80% Max Speed 2: _____	3m

DAY 167	Date __ / __ / ____	
EXERCISE PERMUTATION ASCENDING/DESCENDING	EXERCISE DETAIL and METRONOME SPEED SETTING	TIME
2-3-1-4	Day 2 @ 30% Max Speed 1: _____	3m
4-2-3-1	Day 3 @ 65% Max Speed 1: _____	3m
1-4-2-3	Max Speed 2: _____	
2-1-3-4	Day 1 @ 80% Max Speed 2: _____	3m
4-2-1-3	Day 2 @ 80% Max Speed 2: _____	3m
3-4-2-1	Day 3 @ 80% Max Speed 2: _____	3m
1-3-4-2	Max Speed 3: _____	

DAY 168	Date __ / __ / ____	
EXERCISE PERMUTATION ASCENDING/DESCENDING	EXERCISE DETAIL and METRONOME SPEED SETTING	TIME
2-3-1-4	Day 3 @ 30% Max Speed 1: _____	3m
4-2-3-1	Max Speed 2: _____	
1-4-2-3	Day 1 @ 80% Max Speed 2: _____	3m
2-1-3-4	Day 2 @ 80% Max Speed 2: _____	3m
4-2-1-3	Day 3 @ 80% Max Speed 2: _____	3m
3-4-2-1	Day 4 @ 80% Max Speed 2: _____	3m
1-3-4-2	Day 1 @ 90% Max Speed 3: _____	3m

DAY 169	Date __ / __ / ____	
EXERCISE PERMUTATION ASCENDING/DESCENDING	EXERCISE DETAIL and METRONOME SPEED SETTING	TIME
2-3-1-4	Day 4 @ 30% Max Speed 1: _____	3m
4-2-3-1	Day 1 @ 80% Max Speed 2: _____	3m
1-4-2-3	Day 2 @ 80% Max Speed 2: _____	3m
2-1-3-4	Day 3 @ 80% Max Speed 2: _____	3m
4-2-1-3	Day 4 @ 80% Max Speed 2: _____	3m
3-4-2-1	Day 5 @ 80% Max Speed 2: _____	3m
1-3-4-2	Day 2 @ 90% Max Speed 3: _____	3m

DAY 170	Date __ / __ / ____	
EXERCISE PERMUTATION ASCENDING/DESCENDING	EXERCISE DETAIL and METRONOME SPEED SETTING	TIME
2-3-1-4	Day 5 @ 30% Max Speed 1: _____	3m
4-2-3-1	Day 2 @ 80% Max Speed 2: _____	3m
1-4-2-3	Day 3 @ 80% Max Speed 2: _____	3m
2-1-3-4	Day 4 @ 80% Max Speed 2: _____	3m
4-2-1-3	Day 5 @ 80% Max Speed 2: _____	3m
3-4-2-1	Max Speed 3: _____	
1-3-4-2	Day 3 @ 90% Max Speed 3: _____	3m

DAY 171	Date __ / __ / ____	
EXERCISE PERMUTATION ASCENDING/DESCENDING	EXERCISE DETAIL and METRONOME SPEED SETTING	TIME
2-3-1-4	Day 1 @ 50% Max Speed 1: _____	3m
4-2-3-1	Day 3 @ 80% Max Speed 2: _____	3m
1-4-2-3	Day 4 @ 80% Max Speed 2: _____	3m
2-1-3-4	Day 5 @ 80% Max Speed 2: _____	3m
4-2-1-3	Max Speed 3: _____	
3-4-2-1	Day 1 @ 90% Max Speed 3: _____	3m
1-3-4-2	Day 4 @ 90% Max Speed 3: _____	3m

DAY 172	Date __ /__ /____	
EXERCISE PERMUTATION ASCENDING/DESCENDING	EXERCISE DETAIL and METRONOME SPEED SETTING	TIME
2-3-1-4	Day 2 @ 50% Max Speed 1: _____	3m
4-2-3-1	Day 4 @ 80% Max Speed 2: _____	3m
1-4-2-3	Day 5 @ 80% Max Speed 2: _____	3m
2-1-3-4	Max Speed 3: _____	
4-2-1-3	Day 1 @ 90% Max Speed 3: _____	3m
3-4-2-1	Day 2 @ 90% Max Speed 3: _____	3m
1-3-4-2	Day 5 @ 90% Max Speed 3: _____	3m

DAY 173	Date __ /__ /____	
EXERCISE PERMUTATION ASCENDING/DESCENDING	EXERCISE DETAIL and METRONOME SPEED SETTING	TIME
2-3-1-4	Day 3 @ 50% Max Speed 1: _____	3m
4-2-3-1	Day 5 @ 80% Max Speed 2: _____	3m
1-4-2-3	Max Speed 3: _____	
2-1-3-4	Day 1 @ 90% Max Speed 3: _____	3m
4-2-1-3	Day 2 @ 90% Max Speed 3: _____	3m
3-4-2-1	Day 3 @ 90% Max Speed 3: _____	3m
1-3-4-2	Max Speed 4: _____ Maintenance Level	

DAY 174	Date __ /__ /____	
EXERCISE PERMUTATION ASCENDING/DESCENDING	EXERCISE DETAIL and METRONOME SPEED SETTING	TIME
3-1-4-2	Max Speed 1: _____	
2-3-1-4	Day 1 @ 65% Max Speed 1: _____	3m
4-2-3-1	Max Speed 3: _____	
1-4-2-3	Day 1 @ 90% Max Speed 3: _____	3m
2-1-3-4	Day 2 @ 90% Max Speed 3: _____	3m
4-2-1-3	Day 3 @ 90% Max Speed 3: _____	3m
3-4-2-1	Day 4 @ 90% Max Speed 3: _____	3m

DAY 175	Date __ / __ / ___	
EXERCISE PERMUTATION ASCENDING/DESCENDING	EXERCISE DETAIL and METRONOME SPEED SETTING	TIME
3-1-4-2	Day 1 @ 30% Max Speed 1: _____	3m
2-3-1-4	Day 2 @ 65% Max Speed 1: _____	3m
4-2-3-1	Day 1 @ 90% Max Speed 3: _____	3m
1-4-2-3	Day 2 @ 90% Max Speed 3: _____	3m
2-1-3-4	Day 3 @ 90% Max Speed 3: _____	3m
4-2-1-3	Day 4 @ 90% Max Speed 3: _____	3m
3-4-2-1	Day 5 @ 90% Max Speed 3: _____	3m

DAY 176	Date __ / __ / ___	
EXERCISE PERMUTATION ASCENDING/DESCENDING	EXERCISE DETAIL and METRONOME SPEED SETTING	TIME
3-1-4-2	Day 2 @ 30% Max Speed 1: _____	3m
2-3-1-4	Day 3 @ 65% Max Speed 1: _____	3m
4-2-3-1	Day 2 @ 90% Max Speed 3: _____	3m
1-4-2-3	Day 3 @ 90% Max Speed 3: _____	3m
2-1-3-4	Day 4 @ 90% Max Speed 3: _____	3m
4-2-1-3	Day 5 @ 90% Max Speed 3: _____	3m
3-4-2-1	Max Speed 4: _____ Maintenance Level	

DAY 177	Date __ / __ / ___	
EXERCISE PERMUTATION ASCENDING/DESCENDING	EXERCISE DETAIL and METRONOME SPEED SETTING	TIME
1-4-3-2	Max Speed 1: _____	
3-1-4-2	Day 3 @ 30% Max Speed 1: _____	3m
2-3-1-4	Max Speed 2: _____	
4-2-3-1	Day 3 @ 90% Max Speed 3: _____	3m
1-4-2-3	Day 4 @ 90% Max Speed 3: _____	3m
2-1-3-4	Day 5 @ 90% Max Speed 3: _____	3m
4-2-1-3	Max Speed 4: _____ Maintenance Level	

DAY 178	Date __ / __ / ____	
EXERCISE PERMUTATION ASCENDING/DESCENDING	EXERCISE DETAIL and METRONOME SPEED SETTING	TIME
4-3-2-1	Max Speed 1: _____	
1-4-3-2	Day 1 @ 30% Max Speed 1: _____	3m
3-1-4-2	Day 4 @ 30% Max Speed 1: _____	3m
2-3-1-4	Day 1 @ 80% Max Speed 2: _____	3m
4-2-3-1	Day 4 @ 90% Max Speed 3: _____	3m
1-4-2-3	Day 5 @ 90% Max Speed 3: _____	3m
2-1-3-4	Max Speed 4: _____ Maintenance Level	

DAY 179	Date __ / __ / ____	
EXERCISE PERMUTATION ASCENDING/DESCENDING	EXERCISE DETAIL and METRONOME SPEED SETTING	TIME
3-2-1-4	Max Speed 1: _____	
4-3-2-1	Day 1 @ 30% Max Speed 1: _____	3m
1-4-3-2	Day 2 @ 30% Max Speed 1: _____	3m
3-1-4-2	Day 5 @ 30% Max Speed 1: _____	3m
2-3-1-4	Day 2 @ 80% Max Speed 2: _____	3m
4-2-3-1	Day 5 @ 90% Max Speed 3: _____	3m
1-4-2-3	Max Speed 4: _____ Maintenance Level	

DAY 180	Date __ / __ / ____	
EXERCISE PERMUTATION ASCENDING/DESCENDING	EXERCISE DETAIL and METRONOME SPEED SETTING	TIME
2-1-4-3	Max Speed 1: _____	
3-2-1-4	Day 1 @ 30% Max Speed 1: _____	3m
4-3-2-1	Day 2 @ 30% Max Speed 1: _____	3m
1-4-3-2	Day 3 @ 30% Max Speed 1: _____	3m
3-1-4-2	Day 1 @ 50% Max Speed 1: _____	3m
2-3-1-4	Day 3 @ 80% Max Speed 2: _____	3m
4-2-3-1	Max Speed 4: _____ Maintenance Level	

DAY 181	Date __ / __ / ____	
EXERCISE PERMUTATION ASCENDING/DESCENDING	EXERCISE DETAIL and METRONOME SPEED SETTING	TIME
2-1-4-3	Day 1 @ 30% Max Speed 1: _____	3m
3-2-1-4	Day 2 @ 30% Max Speed 1: _____	3m
4-3-2-1	Day 3 @ 30% Max Speed 1: _____	3m
1-4-3-2	Day 4 @ 30% Max Speed 1: _____	3m
3-1-4-2	Day 2 @ 50% Max Speed 1: _____	3m
2-3-1-4	Day 4 @ 80% Max Speed 2: _____	3m

DAY 182	Date __ / __ / ____	
EXERCISE PERMUTATION ASCENDING/DESCENDING	EXERCISE DETAIL and METRONOME SPEED SETTING	TIME
2-1-4-3	Day 2 @ 30% Max Speed 1: _____	3m
3-2-1-4	Day 3 @ 30% Max Speed 1: _____	3m
4-3-2-1	Day 4 @ 30% Max Speed 1: _____	3m
1-4-3-2	Day 5 @ 30% Max Speed 1: _____	3m
3-1-4-2	Day 3 @ 50% Max Speed 1: _____	3m
2-3-1-4	Day 5 @ 80% Max Speed 2: _____	3m

DAY 183	Date __ / __ / ____	
EXERCISE PERMUTATION ASCENDING/DESCENDING	EXERCISE DETAIL and METRONOME SPEED SETTING	TIME
2-1-4-3	Day 3 @ 30% Max Speed 1: _____	3m
3-2-1-4	Day 4 @ 30% Max Speed 1: _____	3m
4-3-2-1	Day 5 @ 30% Max Speed 1: _____	3m
1-4-3-2	Day 1 @ 50% Max Speed 1: _____	3m
3-1-4-2	Day 1 @ 65% Max Speed 1: _____	3m
2-3-1-4	Max Speed 3: _____	

DAY 184		Date __ / __ / ____
EXERCISE PERMUTATION ASCENDING/DESCENDING	EXERCISE DETAIL and METRONOME SPEED SETTING	TIME
2-1-4-3	Day 4 @ 30% Max Speed 1: _____	3m
3-2-1-4	Day 5 @ 30% Max Speed 1: _____	3m
4-3-2-1	Day 1 @ 50% Max Speed 1: _____	3m
1-4-3-2	Day 2 @ 50% Max Speed 1: _____	3m
3-1-4-2	Day 2 @ 65% Max Speed 1: _____	3m
2-3-1-4	Day 1 @ 90% Max Speed 3: _____	3m

DAY 185		Date __ / __ / ____
EXERCISE PERMUTATION ASCENDING/DESCENDING	EXERCISE DETAIL and METRONOME SPEED SETTING	TIME
2-1-4-3	Day 5 @ 30% Max Speed 1: _____	3m
3-2-1-4	Day 1 @ 50% Max Speed 1: _____	3m
4-3-2-1	Day 2 @ 50% Max Speed 1: _____	3m
1-4-3-2	Day 3 @ 50% Max Speed 1: _____	3m
3-1-4-2	Day 3 @ 65% Max Speed 1: _____	3m
2-3-1-4	Day 2 @ 90% Max Speed 3: _____	3m

DAY 186		Date __ / __ / ____
EXERCISE PERMUTATION ASCENDING/DESCENDING	EXERCISE DETAIL and METRONOME SPEED SETTING	TIME
2-1-4-3	Day 1 @ 50% Max Speed 1: _____	3m
3-2-1-4	Day 2 @ 50% Max Speed 1: _____	3m
4-3-2-1	Day 3 @ 50% Max Speed 1: _____	3m
1-4-3-2	Day 1 @ 65% Max Speed 1: _____	3m
3-1-4-2	Max Speed 2: _____	
2-3-1-4	Day 3 @ 90% Max Speed 3: _____	3m

DAY 187	Date __ / __ / ____	
EXERCISE PERMUTATION ASCENDING/DESCENDING	EXERCISE DETAIL and METRONOME SPEED SETTING	TIME
2-1-4-3	Day 2 @ 50% Max Speed 1: _____	3m
3-2-1-4	Day 3 @ 50% Max Speed 1: _____	3m
4-3-2-1	Day 1 @ 65% Max Speed 1: _____	3m
1-4-3-2	Day 2 @ 65% Max Speed 1: _____	3m
3-1-4-2	Day 1 @ 80% Max Speed 2: _____	3m
2-3-1-4	Day 4 @ 90% Max Speed 3: _____	3m

DAY 188	Date __ / __ / ____	
EXERCISE PERMUTATION ASCENDING/DESCENDING	EXERCISE DETAIL and METRONOME SPEED SETTING	TIME
2-1-4-3	Day 3 @ 50% Max Speed 1: _____	3m
3-2-1-4	Day 1 @ 65% Max Speed 1: _____	3m
4-3-2-1	Day 2 @ 65% Max Speed 1: _____	3m
1-4-3-2	Day 3 @ 65% Max Speed 1: _____	3m
3-1-4-2	Day 2 @ 80% Max Speed 2: _____	3m
2-3-1-4	Day 5 @ 90% Max Speed 3: _____	3m

DAY 189	Date __ / __ / ____	
EXERCISE PERMUTATION ASCENDING/DESCENDING	EXERCISE DETAIL and METRONOME SPEED SETTING	TIME
2-1-4-3	Day 1 @ 65% Max Speed 1: _____	3m
3-2-1-4	Day 2 @ 65% Max Speed 1: _____	3m
4-3-2-1	Day 3 @ 65% Max Speed 1: _____	3m
1-4-3-2	Max Speed 2: _____	
3-1-4-2	Day 3 @ 80% Max Speed 2: _____	3m
2-3-1-4	Max Speed 4: _____ Maintenance Level	

DAY 190	Date __ /__ /____	
EXERCISE PERMUTATION ASCENDING/DESCENDING	EXERCISE DETAIL and METRONOME SPEED SETTING	TIME
2-1-4-3	Day 2 @ 65% Max Speed 1: _____	3m
3-2-1-4	Day 3 @ 65% Max Speed 1: _____	3m
4-3-2-1	Max Speed 2: _____	
1-4-3-2	Day 1 @ 80% Max Speed 2: _____	3m
3-1-4-2	Day 4 @ 80% Max Speed 2: _____	3m

DAY 191	Date __ /__ /____	
EXERCISE PERMUTATION ASCENDING/DESCENDING	EXERCISE DETAIL and METRONOME SPEED SETTING	TIME
2-1-4-3	Day 3 @ 65% Max Speed 1: _____	3m
3-2-1-4	Max Speed 2: _____	
4-3-2-1	Day 1 @ 80% Max Speed 2: _____	3m
1-4-3-2	Day 2 @ 80% Max Speed 2: _____	3m
3-1-4-2	Day 5 @ 80% Max Speed 2: _____	3m

DAY 192	Date __ /__ /____	
EXERCISE PERMUTATION ASCENDING/DESCENDING	EXERCISE DETAIL and METRONOME SPEED SETTING	TIME
2-1-4-3	Max Speed 2: _____	
3-2-1-4	Day 1 @ 80% Max Speed 2: _____	3m
4-3-2-1	Day 2 @ 80% Max Speed 2: _____	3m
1-4-3-2	Day 3 @ 80% Max Speed 2: _____	3m
3-1-4-2	Max Speed 3: _____	

DAY 193	Date __ / __ / ____	
EXERCISE PERMUTATION ASCENDING/DESCENDING	EXERCISE DETAIL and METRONOME SPEED SETTING	TIME
2-1-4-3	Day 1 @ 80% Max Speed 2: _____	3m
3-2-1-4	Day 2 @ 80% Max Speed 2: _____	3m
4-3-2-1	Day 3 @ 80% Max Speed 2: _____	3m
1-4-3-2	Day 4 @ 80% Max Speed 2: _____	3m
3-1-4-2	Day 1 @ 90% Max Speed 3: _____	3m

DAY 194	Date __ / __ / ____	
EXERCISE PERMUTATION ASCENDING/DESCENDING	EXERCISE DETAIL and METRONOME SPEED SETTING	TIME
2-1-4-3	Day 2 @ 80% Max Speed 2: _____	3m
3-2-1-4	Day 3 @ 80% Max Speed 2: _____	3m
4-3-2-1	Day 4 @ 80% Max Speed 2: _____	3m
1-4-3-2	Day 5 @ 80% Max Speed 2: _____	3m
3-1-4-2	Day 2 @ 90% Max Speed 3: _____	3m

DAY 195	Date __ / __ / ____	
EXERCISE PERMUTATION ASCENDING/DESCENDING	EXERCISE DETAIL and METRONOME SPEED SETTING	TIME
2-1-4-3	Day 3 @ 80% Max Speed 2: _____	3m
3-2-1-4	Day 4 @ 80% Max Speed 2: _____	3m
4-3-2-1	Day 5 @ 80% Max Speed 2: _____	3m
1-4-3-2	Max Speed 3: _____	
3-1-4-2	Day 3 @ 90% Max Speed 3: _____	3m

DAY 196	Date __ / __ / ____	
EXERCISE PERMUTATION ASCENDING/DESCENDING	EXERCISE DETAIL and METRONOME SPEED SETTING	TIME
2-1-4-3	Day 4 @ 80% Max Speed 2: _____	3m
3-2-1-4	Day 5 @ 80% Max Speed 2: _____	3m
4-3-2-1	Max Speed 3: _____	3m
1-4-3-2	Day 1 @ 90% Max Speed 3: _____	3m
3-1-4-2	Day 4 @ 90% Max Speed 3: _____	3m

DAY 197	Date __ / __ / ____	
EXERCISE PERMUTATION ASCENDING/DESCENDING	EXERCISE DETAIL and METRONOME SPEED SETTING	TIME
2-1-4-3	Day 5 @ 80% Max Speed 2: _____	3m
3-2-1-4	Max Speed 3: _____	3m
4-3-2-1	Day 1 @ 90% Max Speed 3: _____	3m
1-4-3-2	Day 2 @ 90% Max Speed 3: _____	3m
3-1-4-2	Day 5 @ 90% Max Speed 3: _____	3m

DAY 198	Date __ / __ / ____	
EXERCISE PERMUTATION ASCENDING/DESCENDING	EXERCISE DETAIL and METRONOME SPEED SETTING	TIME
2-1-4-3	Max Speed 3: _____	3m
3-2-1-4	Day 1 @ 90% Max Speed 3: _____	3m
4-3-2-1	Day 2 @ 90% Max Speed 3: _____	3m
1-4-3-2	Day 3 @ 90% Max Speed 3: _____	3m
3-1-4-2	Max Speed 4: _____ Maintenance Level	

DAY 199	Date __ / __ / ____	
EXERCISE PERMUTATION ASCENDING/DESCENDING	EXERCISE DETAIL and METRONOME SPEED SETTING	TIME
2-1-4-3	Day 1 @ 90% Max Speed 3: _____	3m
3-2-1-4	Day 2 @ 90% Max Speed 3: _____	3m
4-3-2-1	Day 3 @ 90% Max Speed 3: _____	3m
1-4-3-2	Day 4 @ 90% Max Speed 3: _____	3m

DAY 200	Date __ / __ / ____	
EXERCISE PERMUTATION ASCENDING/DESCENDING	EXERCISE DETAIL and METRONOME SPEED SETTING	TIME
2-1-4-3	Day 2 @ 90% Max Speed 3: _____	3m
3-2-1-4	Day 3 @ 90% Max Speed 3: _____	3m
4-3-2-1	Day 4 @ 90% Max Speed 3: _____	3m
1-4-3-2	Day 5 @ 90% Max Speed 3: _____	3m

DAY 201	Date __ / __ / ___	
EXERCISE PERMUTATION ASCENDING/DESCENDING	**EXERCISE DETAIL and METRONOME SPEED SETTING**	**TIME**
2-1-4-3	Day 3 @ 90% Max Speed 3: _____	3m
3-2-1-4	Day 4 @ 90% Max Speed 3: _____	3m
4-3-2-1	Day 5 @ 90% Max Speed 3: _____	3m
1-4-3-2	Max Speed 4: _____ Maintenance Level	

DAY 202	Date __ / __ / ___	
EXERCISE PERMUTATION ASCENDING/DESCENDING	**EXERCISE DETAIL and METRONOME SPEED SETTING**	**TIME**
2-1-4-3	Day 4 @ 90% Max Speed 3: _____	3m
3-2-1-4	Day 5 @ 90% Max Speed 3: _____	3m
4-3-2-1	Max Speed 4: _____ Maintenance Level	

DAY 203	Date __ / __ / ___	
EXERCISE PERMUTATION ASCENDING/DESCENDING	**EXERCISE DETAIL and METRONOME SPEED SETTING**	**TIME**
2-1-4-3	Day 5 @ 90% Max Speed 3: _____	3m
3-2-1-4	Max Speed 4: _____ Maintenance Level	

DAY 204	Date __ / __ / ___	
EXERCISE PERMUTATION ASCENDING/DESCENDING	**EXERCISE DETAIL and METRONOME SPEED SETTING**	**TIME**
2-1-4-3	Max Speed 4: _____ Maintenance Level	

DAY 205 – CONGRATUALATIONS!!!
You have completed the entire Daily Burn Program.

I hope you have enjoyed the practice program and have developed and improved your accuracy, dexterity, strength and speed on the guitar. All you need to do now is continue to maintain it!!! It is my sincere wish that you will continue to grow in all aspects of your guitar playing so that you can effectively bring your musical ideas to the guitar, and give the inspiration and gift of music to the world.

Musically,

Christopher Cotter

___

Program Maintenance and Additional Practice Log

To assure that you remain at the optimum levels of accuracy, dexterity, strength, speed, and hand synchronization in all aspects of your guitar playing, you should continue on a maintenance program once you reach completion of a given exercise in the program. Additionally, you can, and should, pick a few exercises in your maintenance program and practice them as warm-ups prior to your daily practices. This is especially important on days in which all of the exercises that day are played at higher speeds.

You can make photocopies of the following log chart and use it for maintenance level exercises and additional program days. You can also download additional Daily Log and Maintenance Log templates at www.jamestownguitars.com.

Daily Practice and Maintenance Log			
DATE	EXERCISE PERMUTATION ASCENDING/DESCENDING	EXERCISE DETAIL and METRONOME SPEED SETTING	TIME

References

Fisher, J. (2010). *Beginning Jazz Guitar*. Van Nuys: Alfred Music Publishing.

Horne, G. (2010). *Beginning Acoustic Guitar*. Van Nuys: Alfred Music Publishing.

Kolb, T. (2010). *Daily Guitar Warm-Ups*. Milwaukee: Hal Leonard.

LaFleur, B. (2006). *Ultimate Guitar Technique*. Milwaukee: Hal Leonard.

Taglirino, B. (2006). *Chord-Tone Soloing*. Milwaukee: Hal Leonard.

Tom Hess Corporation. www.tomhess.net (2002-2014). How to Practice Guitar for Maximum Speed-Part 1. (http://tomhess.net/Articles/HowToPracticeForMaximumSpeedPart1.aspx)

Sudo, P. (1997). *Zen Guitar*. New York: Fireside.